Everyday Kabbalah

Everyday Kabbalah

A Practical Guide to Jewish Meditation, Healing, and Personal Growth

MELINDA RIBNER

A Citadel Press Book
Published by Carol Publishing Group

A Citadel Press Book
Published by Carol Publishing Group
Citadel Press is a registered trademark of Carol Communications, Inc.

Editorial, sales and distribution, rights and permissions inquiries should be
addressed to Carol Publishing Group, 120 Enterprise Avenue, Secaucus, N.J.
07094.

In Canada: Canadian Manda Group, One Atlantic Avenue, Suite 105, Toronto,
Ontario M6K 3E7

Carol Publishing Group books may be purchased in bulk at special discounts for
sales promotion, fundraising, or educational purposes. Special editions can be
created to specifications. For details, contact Special Sales Department, Carol
Publishing Group, 120 Enterprise Avenue, Secaucus, N.J. 07094.

Manufactured in the United States of America
10   9   8   7   6   5   4   3   2   1

Library of Congress Cataloging-in-Publication Data

Ribner, Melinda.
Everyday kabbalah : a practical guide to Jewish meditation,
healing, and personal growth / Melinda Ribner.
p.   cm.
"A Citadel Press book."
ISBN 0-8065-1980-0 (pbk.)
1. Jewish meditations.   2. Spiritual life—Judaism.   3 New Age
movement.   I. Title.
BM724.R53   1998
296.7'2—dc21
98-11413
CIP

To my father of blessed memory, Yitzchok ben Avraham Dovid who showed me that simply being a Jew is holy.

To my sweet family—my mother, my brother, and my uncle—whose love and support is a blessing to me.

To my many teachers, who taught me how to stand before God and reach into heaven for blessings.

To my students, who continually encouraged me to teach, to grow, and to transcend what I thought was possible for myself.

There are thousands of ways to meditate, but in reality little has been done for the English brothers and sisters to give them a taste of what Jewish meditation is all about, what our holy rabbis have been teaching all their lives. Jewish meditation is not just a way to be more centered or balanced, it is much deeper. Prayer is the time when I speak to God as the master of the world. Meditation is when it is clear to me that God is my best friend. God is closer to me than my own breath. Mindy is one of those special human beings who never forgets there is one God. She has the privilege of bringing these deep teachings to the English-speaking public. Her meditations go straight to the heart of every person.

—Rabbi Shlomo Carlebach of Blessed Memory

Contents

Part II: Meditations for Self-Healing

Preface

I hope that this book will uplift, heal, and transform you in the way that you most want for yourself. It is my prayer that your relationship with God will be deeper and that you will have more love, joy, well-being, and purpose in your life as a result of your involvement in Jewish meditation. I believe that meditation is truly the greatest gift you can give yourself. Its value will increase with time and practice.

The material for this book comes from my experience of teaching beginning Jewish meditation for over fourteen years, and from my experience as a psychotherapist incorporating meditation as a treatment modality. My classes in Jewish meditation are attended by Jews from every affiliation of Judaism—Chassidic, Orthodox, Conservative, Reform, Reconstructionist, and Jewish renewal, as well as secular Jews, Jews affiliated with Yogic or Buddhist paths, and non-Jews interested in kabbalah.

My purpose in writing this book is to spare you some of the hard work and lonely searching I had to do until I found Jewish meditation. When I began my spiritual search, information about Jewish meditation was not available in English. I was typical of many who turned to Eastern meditation for personal growth, spirituality, and a sense of community. Many of us baby boomers recall that, when we were growing up, the synagogues and Hebrew schools were not exactly bastions of love and spirituality. We may have longed for spirituality, for connection with the Divine, yet found only politics, fundraising, and gossiping during prayer services.

As a child, I noticed during services that no one appeared to be praying. I wondered what we were all doing there. The experience felt so empty. The synagogue seemed mostly like a social club, an opportunity to see and be seen by other people. It was often so for me and my girlfriends as children and teenagers; we often didn't make it to the inside of the sanctuary. I remember, however, as a child, wishing deep inside that I knew how to pray and could be in a synagogue where everyone knew how to pray. I knew intuitively that this would be very beautiful.

Because my father came from an Orthodox background, my mother came from a Reform background, and I attended a Conservative Hebrew school, I had the opportunity to pray in all three synagogues. They all seemed the same to me. After my bat mitzvah, I stopped my Jewish learning, but remained active in various Jewish youth groups. I was even President of the Albany Jewish Youth Council in my senior year of high school. I felt a very strong identification as a Jew, and planned to live in Israel after college.

My involvement in Jewish life was suspended during my college years. Meeting and living with people who were quite different from me made me question the way I had lived my life. I remember feeling like a farm girl from Idaho next to the sophisticated Jews from New York City. My values were challenged. I was for the first time confronted with promiscuity, drugs, nude-ins, and a variety of alternative lifestyles and ideologies.

I became confused about who I really was. What did I really believe? Was I simply a product of my parental, societal, or peer values, or did I have a more transcendental, more essential, inner self? Why was I born? What was my purpose? What is life? Was there a God? I was haunted by those deep existential questions of life. My life felt like an existential question. Even though I was very popular in college, even though I had a date every night and many boyfriends, I was lonely and troubled. Taking courses in sociology and philosophy only added to my anxiety and discomfort. Therapy offered me no relief. I read spiritual books of all sorts, but they seemed too abstract to me. In my despair and loneliness, I called out to God and began to meditate on my own.

The first time I sat for meditation, I heard an angelic voice. It was very beautiful; however, I was frightened by it. Today it is popular to talk about encounters with angels, but when this happened to me, nobody talked about such experiences. I was ashamed to tell anyone about it; I thought I was going crazy. Yet the voice was reassuring, and has continued to be a source of comfort for me. Years later I received confirmation that this voice was authentic. My inner life was rich, deep, and very intense. I was often overwhelmed by the spiritual experiences I had. To calm myself, I would write beautiful poetry and prayers to God that I saved through all the moving around I have done since college. It is interesting for me to read the poems I wrote at the start of my spiritual quest. They still speak to me today. They are dear to me because they are the outpourings of my soul before I had exposure to any gurus, rabbis, or even Jewish books. I would like to share one of these prayer-poems I wrote in college.

I tremble before you, God, fearing my insignificant doubts may make me unworthy. My fears diminish before me while I meditate on Your mercy and great love, realizing that I am not here on my own accord, therefore have no right to judge myself. In the darkness, may the light of Your Presence illuminate my soul and the souls of all living creatures. And let these shimmering hidden flames rekindle each other, nourishing while remembering always the source of it all. Let all have a thread of the Holy Blanket, for without a flame or a thread, the world is too cold.

Help me to put my trust completely in You. For it has been in those moments I have found peace. Help me to yearn for You as if my whole being rests with You.

For only in the yearning have I learned to listen, accept, wait, and be found by You.

For without You, life is a cheap marketplace, a sham, a nightmare. No, such life is unimaginable

I went to my Hillel rabbi, hoping that I would find someone to talk to about God and the meaning of life. He told me not to think so much and to take up swimming. I did not take up swimming, but a guru from India came to my college and spoke about God, love, and how to live a meaningful life. Finally, someone was answering my questions. I loved the chanting and meditation that were part of the gatherings with the guru. I discovered the dynamic prayer life I had yearned for since I was a child.

After graduation, I lived in two different ashrams, where I did intense meditation and other spiritual practices for several years. Living in an ashram was a little like being in the army. In one ashram, I shared a small room with three other women. I slept in the lower bunk. We arose at five in the morning, and lights were out in our room at nine-thirty at night. There was even an ex–marine sergeant, also a resident, who checked our beds for creases and occasionally did roll call during morning prayers. Though the discipline was difficult, I felt stronger and happier than ever before. I spent six hours each day in prayer and meditation. I often had ecstatic experiences in meditation. I understood spiritual teachings on a deeper level. Some of these experiences awakened me to Judaism and Torah. God became a very real and continual presence in my life.

While living in an ashram in Manhattan, I would sometimes spend Saturdays in intensive meditation programs where we would chant and meditate the entire day and evening. These times were particularly other-worldly, wonderful, and powerful. Sometimes I

was filled with such bliss and rapture that I thought I might leave this
world right then with a smile on my face. Even so, when I would
walk outside at lunchtime and see Jews returning from synagogue, I
would cry. I wanted to be a part of them. They represented to me the
holiness of this world. I began to attend synagogue while living in
the ashram. On regular Saturdays when there was not a meditation
intensive, I would arise at five in the morning, do my ashram
chanting and meditation till nine in the morning, and then go to
Rabbi Shlomo Carlebach's synagogue for morning and afternoon
services.

By going to synagogue, I became aware that I might be following
another religion at the ashram. I don't know why I did not know that
at first. Perhaps it was because the ashram was so filled with spiritual
Jewish seekers like myself, it felt like a Jewish place. We used to joke
that if not for the guru we would have a *minyan*, a quota of people
required for prayer according to Jewish law. So even though I was
singing prayers in Sanskrit, learning Vedanta and Kashmir Shavism
philosophies, and even, on occasion, wearing beautiful saris and
sporting a red dot on the middle of my forehead, it did not dawn on
me that I was following another religion. When friends began to take
vows of renunciation, wear orange clothes, and be called swami, it
really began to seem like another religion, but I was told repeatedly
that it was not. It was not until I visited home and my father opened
the encyclopedia to the section on Hinduism that I realized, much to
my surprise, that I was familiar with everything that was discussed. I
knew all the Sanskrit terms, and then some. I had been praying in
Sanskrit for over a year.

I instantly realized that I was following an Americanized form of
Hinduism. Even though I was upset about this, as it was never my
intention to practice another religion, I continued to stay in the
ashram rationalizing my involvement and suppressing my increasing
inner conflicts regarding Eastern meditation practices and Judaism.
"Isn't there one God? Does it really matter how I connect to God?" It

was very hard for me to leave the ashram, on so many levels. I loved the community life. I loved the meditation. I loved the teachers. I had good friends. I was very much in love with a man I had met on the day that I had also met the guru. I thought that this man was my soulmate. Though he came from an ultra-religious background and had been in yeshiva until he was twenty-two years old, he was annoyed by my interest in Judaism and tried to discourage me.

Finally, when I attended my grandfather's funeral a few months later, I discovered the determination to move out of the ashram. During the eulogy, the rabbi seemed to read out of a rabbi's handbook, words he most likely had said at so many funerals before: "He leaves behind a lineage of devout Jews." I remember that the family members looked at each other sheepishly, wondering who were these devout Jews he was talking about. But deep inside, at that very moment, I decided that I wanted to be that Jew. I did not want to break the chain of the Jewish people. I did not want my grandfather to have to answer in heaven for a Hindu granddaughter. I would be as whole-hearted about Judaism as I had been about Yoga. It was this promise that I made to myself, to my grandfather, and to God at my grandfather's funeral that kept me connected to Judaism through all the challenges I would face.

I returned from the funeral, and moved out of the ashram that very day. Miraculously, there was a space in a beautiful apartment nearby with ashram disciples. The next Saturday, I started to observe the Sabbath. When I began to take on Judaism, I did not know exactly what being observant meant. I learned over time, and I still do. Because I had come to appreciate the structure and discipline of a spiritual life from living in the ashram, I was eager to find a comparable Jewish practice. I wanted my life to be permeated with the awareness of God's presence. I hoped and prayed that Judaism would support me in this way. During that time, particularly, I could not help but sense my grandfather's soul guiding my steps back to Judaism.

Almost immediately, with the help of a practical manual about keeping Shabbos, I began to make Shabbos meals for the non-Jewish ashram friends with whom I was living. I learned all the blessings, and incorporated meditations into the meal. These were wonderful times for all of us. Shabbos was like a meditation intensive each week. We meditated before, during, and after the meal.

When I eventually began to meet more observant Jews, I was invited to their homes for Shabbos meals. I was surprised to find that people talked during the meal, even about mundane things. This was painful for me. My Shabbos experience was diminished. Eventually, I got used to having conversation during meals, but I never lost the hunger for meditative Shabbos meals.

Over the next few years, I became increasingly involved in Judaism; however, I did not entirely relinquish my connection to the ashram. I would run from the synagogue to the ashram and back to the synagogue. I still did the meditation techniques I learned at the ashram. I was very much into comparing what I knew about both of them. I felt that I had a unique perspective because I knew both paths intimately. I was disappointed to hear from my gurus and my rabbis that I had to choose one path to follow. "Isn't there one God? Aren't all paths taking a person to the same oneness? Can't I take a little from this path, and a little from another? Can't I be a religious Jew and still do Eastern meditation?"

When I was in the throes of my conflict between Judaism and Yoga, I came across an article of an interview with Reb Shlomo where he said that comparing spiritual paths was like two men comparing their wives. Such comparisons do not make sense if the men really love their wives. The more a man loves his wife, the less he can say about her. He is not interested in comparing her to another. It's private. It's sacred. Being on a particular spiritual path is like being married. It requires fidelity.

I was warned by one of the gurus that if I did not choose one path, I would be like a person standing with one foot in two boats. I would soon fall into the water and be left with nothing. My ashram friends were bewildered that I would consider leaving the protection of an enlightened powerful master. My Jewish friends warned me that I was violating one of the Ten Commandments—the one against idolatry, a serious sin. I was confused and pained. Inside, I felt myself to be universalistic and by nature eclectic. On my own, I would embrace all religions and spiritual paths. Yet I was being forced to choose. Because of my vow at my grandfather's funeral, I couldn't *not* be Jewish.

My final break with Eastern meditation came in 1982, when I attended a conference on transpersonal psychology in Bombay. It was quite a spiritual extravaganza. My rabbis Shlomo Carlebach and Zalman Schachter-Shalomi and one of my gurus, Swami Muktananda, as well as Mother Teresa, the Dalai Lama, and many other leading teachers in personal growth and spirituality, were there. There were so many wonderful people from all over the world. It was thrilling and transformational. There was such a tremendous feeling of oneness, such high spiritual energy at the conference, we felt as if we were ushering in a time of greater spiritual consciousness for the entire world. It definitely was a taste of the World to Come.

While I was in India I had the opportunity to visit the Jewish community of Bombay with Rabbis Shlomo Carlebach and Zalman Schachter-Shalomi for an evening concert. There I saw people who looked like Indians who were wearing Indian clothes, but their names were Avraham, Sarah, Yehudit, Yosef. My concept of what was Jewish instantly expanded. Forgive my ignorance and lack of experience at that time, but somehow I had thought that all Jews were fair-skinned, looking and sounding somewhat like American and Israeli Jews. Now, in India, as I sang and danced with these Indian Jews, it was clear to me that Judaism was an ancient and universal religion that transcended race and nationality. When I spoke to these Indian Jews, I realized that they had the same concerns and the same dreams as the Jews I had met in New York. They were even more hungry for Torah and Jewish spirituality. Here they were in India, such a small minority, so dedicated to maintaining their Jewishness. I was inspired and proud.

While in India, I also stayed for a week in an ashram. It was an exotic and beautiful palace. Within the ashram were various temples housing gold statues of the previous guru, along with the statues of elephant and monkey gods. To my surprise, there were also living "holy" cows that actually roamed wherever they pleased. It was very Indian. I was uncomfortable with all the statues. Even though I slept in a room with about a hundred women, I was very lonely at the ashram. I barely had the opportunity to say hello to the women who were sleeping less than an arm's length away from me. Everyone was so busy meditating, working, or sleeping. In such a spiritual place of thousands of people, there was no one for me to talk to about my feelings about being there. It all seemed very impersonal.

As a visitor to the ashram, I was expected to do a few hours of service for the community. I was assigned to dishwashing in the kitchen after lunch. Much to my surprise, the kitchen was filled with Israelis. I was the only American there. All I heard during that time was Hebrew. I wondered why people from Israel, which I considered the spiritual center of the world, came to India. Why couldn't these beautiful people find spiritual nourishment in Judaism? It was very strange. I felt great pain for the Jewish people. Not only did we as a people have to go through the Holocaust, but here we were, the next generation of Jews, washing dishes in India. The whole experience made me more hungry and desperate for Judaism and Israel.

Being in India was disillusioning. I had to be in India to see how the spiritual philosophy of Hinduism supported the poverty of the people. I was appalled. How convenient to say that this world is an illusion, or that people suffer because it is their karma. I knew in my heart that such poverty would never be tolerated by Jewish people.

Judaism emphasizes each person's responsibility to fix the world. During that visit, it became clear to me that I needed to stop meditating with an Eastern mantra.

A few months later I went to Israel to immerse myself in Jewish learning. I wanted to enter into the purest essence of Judaism. I increased my religious practice. I prayed three times a day and made my prayers a meditative experience. I recited additional psalms each day at the Western Wall, Judaism's holiest site. I went to special women's yeshivot, places of learning for those returning to Judaism. This was also very hard for me. The Judaism they taught at these yeshivot was very different from what I had previously experienced with Reb Shlomo. The yeshivot seemed to me like factories for turning out religious conformists as quickly as possible. They wanted me to act and dress in a certain way, forget who I had been before, and not think too much. I felt a subtle message that I should not even ask questions; I might embarrass the teacher, who couldn't respond, or I would be labeled a heretic. I felt that these teachers were interested not in feeding my soul, but only in having me conform to their view of reality.

My stay in Israel in the early 1980s was also greatly affected by the tense political climate of the country at that time. I was there before a major election. Bomb threats were almost a daily occurrence. Many Shabbos meals were roundtables of political discussion rather than the spiritual meditative experiences I had grown to love with Reb Shlomo. My universalistic loving spirit was stifled. I was in great despair about my ability to grow spiritually in a Jewish framework. I even questioned my desire to be Jewish at all. It seemed like a heavy karma. I somehow understood why the Israelis I had met in India were so happy washing dishes in India. Life was simple. These people probably couldn't bear the divisiveness in the Jewish community. I also wanted to escape. It wasn't that my religious observance was being questioned. I still wanted to be religious; that was between me and God. I was happy about my relationship with

God, I just wasn't sure about being part of this Jewish community.
Was I strong enough to love these difficult people? Would I have to
suffer because of their hatred and narrow-mindedness? At my darkest
moment, as I was planning my escape to Nepal, I was invited to join
a small experiential group of people learning Jewish meditation. This
was not my first encounter with Jewish meditation. I had been
exposed to Jewish meditation earlier during my transition period to
Judaism, but it was watered-down compared to what I had
experienced in the ashram. I was not interested in a weak imitation.

My experience in this Jewish meditation group, however, was
different. The teacher, a man from the Midwest who had previously
spent many years in Nepal and India practicing Buddhism, was very
skilled in guiding meditation. He, like the others in the group, had
come to Jerusalem in search of a spiritual awakening. With the help
of translated manuscripts, we began to explore kabbalistic
meditation. I dropped out of yeshiva, devoting my time to learning
massage, kabbalah, and meditation. I also began attending the
kabbalah classes of Rabbi Yitzchok Ginzberg, who was teaching
men and women at the time. Many things happened to me during
this visit that I had never anticipated or imagined. It was
challenging, yet God gave me exactly what I needed to grow
spiritually and Jewishly. It was not mainstream or what I had
planned.

When I returned to New York, a women's yeshiva had just opened
up a few blocks from my home. I began learning with Rabbi
Yitzchok Kirzner. Here, finally, was a person who asked deep
questions of life and honored the questions I asked. I knew from the
first class that I was in the presence of a great and lofty soul. Rabbi
Kirzner gave me a solid foundation in Judaism. He introduced me to
the classics of Jewish philosophy, books written by the Rambam, the
Ramchal, Rabbenu Yonah. For years I studied with him the book,
Duties of the Heart by Ibn Paquda. This book, which I had stumbled
upon while browsing in a Jewish bookstore right after my

grandfather's funeral, had placed me on the path to religious observance. After learning with Rabbi Kirzner for several years, I discovered, much to my surprise, that I had had a dream about him years before I met him. In the dream, he was an interior decorator working for the Salvation Army, and we had a deep discussion about what it meant to trust in God. I recorded the dream in detail. I was grateful that I had the opportunity to read Rabbi Kirzner this dream from my dream book, and tell him that he was my interior decorator, two months before he passed away at the age of forty in 1991.

Rabbi Shlomo Carlebach was my primary teacher. I learned with Reb Shlomo for almost twenty years. He was my actual entry into Judaism. Though Shlomo was a door to Judaism for thousands of people, I was one of the few who stayed with him. I worked for Shlomo for many years. He was my "guru" replacement. He affectionately called me his "right hand." For years, I organized classes and concerts for him. To support his spiritual teaching, I cooked Shabbos and holiday meals for hundreds of people. Shabbos meals with Reb Shlomo would sometimes last for eight hours. Those who were privileged to *daven* with Reb Shlomo once or twice can imagine how blessed I was to have *davened* with him for twenty years. Every Shabbos, every holiday, every learning session with him was thrilling. Reb Shlomo taught me how to transcend myself, enter paradise, and return with blessings. I also learned how to teach others to do this for themselves. Though Reb Shlomo would always tell everyone that they were sweet like sugar or holy, one of the greatest compliments Reb Shlomo paid me in all the years of praying with him was to say that he was aware of me when he prayed.

After I was with Reb Shlomo for thirteen years, he offered me a *smeicha*—an ordination to teach Jewish meditation. This move was somewhat radical, as Shlomo was an Orthodox rabbi, and women are not given such public endorsement. The *smeicha*, however, was non-rabbinical. When I received the actual *smeicha* from Reb Shlomo, it was very powerful. I felt him become a conduit for the blessings of all the holy rebbes he so frequently talked about. In that fleeting moment, which felt like eternity, I became a Jew and a teacher on a different level. Judaism entered my cells, the pores of my body. I was plugged in in a new and deeper way.

Even before he gave me *smeicha*, Reb Shlomo invited me to teach meditation at his shul. I began guiding meditation before morning and afternoon services on Shabbos and teaching one night a week. I was soon invited to teach at a popular Orthodox synagogue, Lincoln Square Synagogue; a conservative synagogue, Ansche Chesed; and a Reform synagogue, Rodeph Sholom.

After teaching at these synagogues for a few years, each one on a different night of the week, many of the students at each place wanted to continue and deepen their experiences in meditation. I brought them all together and formed The Jewish Meditation Circle, which offers weekly classes, special events, and New Moon celebrations. Several of these students have been with me since the beginning. Having a continuous weekly group of devoted students for about ten years has encouraged me to grow in the most wonderful ways. We truly have been pioneers in accessing the depths of meditation and kabbalah. Our sessions are exciting, unique, and ecstatic. This book is an introduction to this work.

I feel vulnerable at having shared such intimate details of my spiritual journey. Though I am an open-hearted person, I am also very private. Much of this information will be new to my friends and students. I share in this way because I imagine that you may have questions about who I am and how I became a teacher of Jewish meditation. I also suspect that many of my readers will be able to relate to aspects of my spiritual journey, and that my sharing may inspire you to go forward in Jewish meditation. By revealing myself in this fashion, I also want to encourage people to be spiritually intimate with each other.

At this point in my life, I feel that everything that has happened to me has brought me closer to God and has made me a better person, a better therapist, and a better Jewish meditation teacher. Ultimately I see that everything has been for good, even all the challenging, painful life experiences. Perhaps I learned the most from them. I feel much gratitude to God for enabling me both to practice and teach Jewish meditation and to write this book

Introduction

Many people today are intrigued by kabbalah, but they do not know what it is. Sometimes people tell me that they are interested in kabbalah, but not in Judaism. This is ironic, as kabbalah is an essential part of Judaism. I do not believe that it can or ought be separated from Judaism. Kabbalah literally means "to receive." Kabbalah is a part of the Torah that Moses received on Mount Sinai. Within kabbalah, there are three branches of knowledge. There is the theoretical kabbalah, which explains the mysteries of God, creation, and the Bible. There is meditative kabbalah, which reveals the meditative techniques to obtain high states of spiritual awareness. And there is practical kabbalah, which illuminates the techniques and practices to achieve particular goals and objectives in the physical world.

In my estimation, kabbalah is the basics of Judaism. Kabbalah is the soul of Judaism. People may question how you can learn kabbalah if you do not know the basics of Judaism. Many people, turned off by the simple teachings of Judaism, require deeper kabbalistic teachings to make a connection with Judaism and Jewish practice. Meditation and kabbalah may be exactly what your soul needs to grow. The study of kabbalah without a grounding in Jewish thought and practice, however, is like a soul without a body. For this reason I have taken the time to explain, incorporate, and transmit basic Jewish teachings through various guided meditation experiences.

You will find that this work remains within the parameters of traditional Judaism. This does not mean that what I present will not be new, exciting, and creative. Just because something is based on something traditional does not mean that it cannot also be personally and currently relevant. The durability and power of Judaism rests on its capacity to be dynamic, to have both constancy and permeability. Regardless of your ideology, whether you are to the left or to the right in Jewish thought and practice, you most likely will be challenged by the ideas and practices given in this book, but therein will be your greatest growth. I have personally found that in learning about and practicing Judaism, as well as in other areas of my life, the areas where I have had the most resistance, the most challenge, have provided the greatest opening and transformation.

Some of you will object to the continual references to God as masculine, which I do throughout this book. Please do not allow the gender references to be a barrier for you. God is not male, God is not female, God is not human, God is not physical. The Bible may speak of God as if He were physical—with a hand, a foot, an eye; as if He had human emotions, like pleasure or anger. God is not even spiritual. Our tendency to make God in our own image so that we can relate to Him causes some confusion for many. As we learn more kabbalah, many of these problems will be clarified. Please be patient. It is good to remember the words of Rabbi Levi Yitzchok of Berditchev, who once said to a self-proclaimed atheist, "The God you don't believe in, I also don't believe in." People usually rebel against their own limited concept of God, not against God. Some people, when they hear the word God, can't help but think of an old man on a throne with a long white beard. Often, people who have trouble with the word God prefer using terms like Higher Power, Universal Consciousness, or Cosmic Energy. That is fine. Judaism has always had many names for the Divine.

In the course of life, we all have made decisions about ourselves, God, and Judaism that limit us. Sometimes the decisions we made in childhood continue to guide us as adults, even though they may no longer be appropriate. For example, I have had many students who deprived themselves of the richness of a Jewish life because they had negative experiences in synagogue as children. This is unfortunate. We need to recognize that we, as adults, have the capacity to experience God, Judaism, and life in a way very different from when we were children. This, however, takes the willingness to examine and let go of limiting ideas of God, and even of who we are, and do the necessary healing so that we may open to greater truth and reality.

All the meditations in this book are healing and therapeutic. Some are designed to give spiritual fortitude to particular challenges we all may face sometime in our lives. Though meditation has a therapeutic component to it, it is not the same as therapy. In traditional therapy we also may become aware of our inner blocks, our limiting ideas, and the ways we have sabotaged ourselves; however, traditional therapy does not address the divine dimension of a person's being, the soul and its needs. It is not within the training of the therapist to heal a person's relationship with God. This is a difference of great magnitude. The therapist cannot instruct the client in how to avail himself of divine assistance. Jewish meditation will do these things. God is a master therapist and healer. His rates are reasonable, and He is always available for an appointment.

Furthermore, I have found that the emotional release a person experiences in meditation generally does not leave the emotional residue that may result in a therapy session. Because meditation enables a person to access his own soul and receive Divine support, he can transcend limiting ego concepts of self more easily and experience his true feelings more deeply. Meditation is an effective treatment modality particularly helpful for people who are verbal or analytical or who use words in therapy to avoid internal expression of feelings. I work with people in my private practice who are also in traditional psychoanalytical therapy. Meditation is a wonderful complement to therapy.

PART I

Beginning Jewish Meditation

1

The Journey That Will
Change Your Life

Everyday Kabbalah is a spiritual journey into the depths of who you are. It is not simply to be read, but to be experienced. Implicit is the recognition that a big difference exists between knowing something intellectually and knowing it experientially; that is, knowing something in such a way that it is integrated into your being. Many more erudite, eloquent, and brilliant spiritual books are now available, but they may not empower you the way this book will. Knowledge without application, without integration, may be interesting, but it is basically irrelevant. If you read this book and are the same as you were before, then it need not have been written, and you did not need to read it. *Everyday Kabbalah* will make a difference in your life. The impact it will have on you will be in proportion to the level of your participation in the meditations and exercises provided. If you are sincere and dedicated, you will reap many extraordinary benefits.

Everyday Kabbalah is a systematic how-to manual in Jewish

meditation that is easily accessible, regardless of your background and experience. It introduces you to the teachings and the meditative and spiritual practices of the *musar,* Chassidic, and kabbalistic schools of Judaism. It also includes instruction in powerful breathing, relaxation, visualization, and transpersonal exercises to integrate spiritual principles directly into your life. Synthesizing breathing and relaxation practices with kabbalistic knowledge and practices is a particularly powerful combination.

Everyday Kabbalah should be acceptable to everyone regardless of previous belief, background, or experience. It is not necessary that you be Jewish. Whatever differences we may have in ideology or background pales in the light of all we share as human beings. The approach of this book is to support your growth wherever you are. Whether you are a novice in meditation and spirituality or a long-time practitioner of Jewish spirituality or any meditative or religious discipline, this book is for you. If you are a spiritual person who avoids contact with organized religion, dogma, or conformity, this book is especially for you.

The seasoned spiritual seekers reading this book have already experimented with many different kinds of personal growth therapies. Many of you, like me, have done gestalt, psychoanalysis, psychosynthesis, the Forum, and so on. Some of us have even traveled to Tibet, India, Japan, and many other places in search of spiritual knowledge, only to be told to meditate, to look within. To receive instruction in meditation, we found ourselves attending ashrams or zendos, learning the philosophies and practicing the rituals of the religious tradition from which the meditative practices were derived. We have been Yogis, Buddhists, and Sufis. We have followed the Course in Miracles. Several months ago, on a bus, I met a Jewish woman who had lived in Nepal for over twenty-five years, practicing and now teaching Buddhism. She confided to me that if she had had access to kabbalah and Jewish meditation, she would have stayed closer to home. She is typical of many Jews practicing, and even teaching, Eastern forms of meditation.

Many of us feel that we benefited from participation in Eastern meditation. We may have tasted great spiritual bliss and a deepening understanding of truth and reality. We may have experienced the joy of belonging to a spiritual community, yet deep inside, in our heart of hearts, some of us do not feel totally comfortable traveling down another spiritual path. Even after many years, we still may be uncomfortable chanting in Sanskrit the names of various gods and goddesses, even though we have become adept at rationalizing this practice.

A popular story attributed to Rabbi Nachman, a spiritual master of the eighteenth century, provides an important teaching.

A man named Moshe from the city of Chernovitz had a recurrent dream that a treasure chest of riches was buried near the steps to a particular bridge in St. Petersburg. He initially dismissed the dream; however, when the dream persisted for a week, he decided to journey there. As he was not a rich man, the journey posed a great hardship for him. Still, he went.

When he finally arrived in St. Petersburg, he soon saw the very bridge that was in his dream. Next to the steps to the bridge stood a policeman. At that time, Jews were not allowed in St. Petersburg without a special business permit. Moshe waited for the officer to leave. The officer, noticing him loitering in the area, asked him why he was in St. Petersburg. Moshe told him about his dream, how he saw this very bridge, and that a treasure was buried under it. He even offered to share the treasure with him. The officer laughed and laughed, telling him that he was a fool to follow crazy dreams. "Do you know," he told the Jew, "I also have a dream that keeps coming back to me every night. In my dream there is a Jew called Moshe from the city of Chernovitz, and under his stove

a buried treasure." The officer smirked. "You don't see me
...ing there." Moshe was startled, and then quickly excused
himself and sped home. He found the buried treasure under his
own stove.

Like Dorothy in *The Wizard of Oz*, we have traveled to many
faraway places, and we now want to come home. We wonder where
home is. Is there anything there for us? We may have been turned off
by earlier contacts with Judaism. So many of us have been deprived
of the most elementary and basic teachings about Judaism; yet we
hope, deep inside, that we will find what we are looking for in our
own spiritual background. Like Moshe, our travels have not been in
vain. Everything has brought us to where we are now. It most likely
was necessary that we search, travel, and explore in the ways we did.
We learned many important things that have prepared us for this
journey in Jewish meditation.

Others of us have stayed closer to home. We long for spirituality,
but do not know where to look. We have not traveled to faraway
places; we have sought happiness and our sense of self in material
acquisition, career, and relationships. We keep thinking that more
will make us happy; perhaps with a larger house, more children,
more money, we will be secure and finally happy. Some of us may
have all the money we need and much love in our life, but still not
feel fulfilled. It is not that the blessings of the physical world are not
important to us, but we wonder if that is all there is.

Others of us have not been successful in realizing our personal
goals. We do not have that great job or that wonderful relationship.
We have experienced unusual hardships. We wonder whether we are
destined to be miserable or wounded for our entire lives. What is it
that really makes a person happy? Why is it that some people who
have so little can be content? To reflect on this question, we need a
Chassidic story.

One day, a very wealthy man came to a rebbe and asked him, "How can a person be happy in the midst of suffering? I have all the wealth I need and I am still not happy." The rebbe said to him, "To learn the answer to this question, you will have to see Reb Zusya" (an eighteenth-century mystic who is a beloved character of many Chassidic stories). The rebbe gave him the directions to Reb Zusya's home. The rich man traveled there and came upon a very disheveled, broken-down house. He thought, "This can't be the home of Reb Zusya. How can a person live in such a dwelling?" Yet it must be, so he knocked at the door. Reb Zusya answered and identified himself. The rich man explained that he was sent by the rebbe to find out how a person can be happy in the midst of suffering. Reb Zusya replied, "I do not know why the rebbe sent you to me. I never had a bad day in my life."

How can we be like Reb Zusya? Reb Zusya was one of those special people who lived in the constant awareness of God.

We all want to be content and happy with our lives. This is a natural desire. Many of us have come to realize that our happiness is fragile if it is dependent on something physical or transitory. At times, we sense that what occurs within us is more important than what we have and what we do. We need and want to find happiness within ourselves. For this reason we turn to meditation. However varied our background and life experience, we now turn to Jewish meditation. We want to experience all the benefits of meditation that we have heard about, or even experienced before, in an Eastern discipline.

The prophet Isaiah predicts a time when "There will be a thirst and hunger in the land but the thirst will not be for water and the hunger will not be for bread, but to hear the word of God." The kabbalists of old declared that some day in the future the masses would seek the profound spirituality and wisdom of meditation and kabbalah. They foresaw that previous restrictions about the dissemination of this knowledge would be lifted at that time. Perhaps this is the time. With an increased interest in spirituality becoming apparent in the general public, many believe that we are living in very auspicious times. There is greater openness and willingness than ever before to reveal the inner wisdom of the Jewish mystical tradition known as kabbalah to a public which has, up to now been deprived of these rich teachings and practices. Only in the last fifteen years has the English-speaking public been informed about the existence of Jewish meditation. In the 1970s and 1980s, Rabbi Aryeh Kaplan and Rabbi Louis Jacobs pioneered this effort by writing a number of books on Jewish meditation. I heard at a lecture in the mid-1980s by Dr. Moshe Idel, a professor of kabbalah at Hebrew University in Jerusalem, that a decision had recently been made among the religious kabbalistic community to allow manuscripts of kabbalah and Jewish meditation to be published in both Hebrew and English. This decision was made in response to the large numbers of Jews becoming involved in Eastern meditation. It was hoped that, having the information about kabbalah and meditation, Jews would soon recognize that their spiritual needs could be met within Judaism. Rav Avraham Yitzchok Kook, the first Chief Rabbi of Israel, also a great kabbalist, predicted that there would be a thirst for meditation and kabbalah in people estranged from traditional Judaism. He advised that this calling of the soul be honored. The late Lubavitcher Rebbe, one of the foremost religious leaders of our time, issued a call for Jewish meditation in the 1980s. Rabbi Zalman Schachter-Shalomi responded to the need for Jewish meditation and accessible Jewish spirituality for many Jewish practitioners of Eastern meditation and others who felt isolated from the Jewish establishment. He initiated the Jewish renewal movement, which incorporates meditation into its prayer services.

Why Now?

To understand why this interest occurs now, we need to understand and appreciate the scope of the devastation of the Holocaust. In addition to the tragedy of the tremendous loss of Jewish lives and the horror of how they died, the Jewish community suffered a loss in faith and spirituality. We lost our greatest and most holy teachers, who would have inspired and guided us. It was hard for many to believe in a loving personal God after the Holocaust. Many Jews chose not to affiliate with Judaism at all, questioning the efficacy of Jewish identification. It was not safe to be too obviously Jewish. Some even feared for the safety of their children and did not even inform them of their Jewish identity. I have been very surprised to have had a number of students in their late thirties or their forties, raised as Americans, who only just found out they were born of Jewish parents or grandparents. This phenomenon is also occurring in Eastern Europe. When Reb Shlomo went to Poland, he met hundreds of Jews whose lives were spared because they were raised in Catholic monasteries as Catholics. They are now very curious about Judaism. Even with all the problems of being a Jewish state, the existence of Israel has given Jews a measure of security and pride in being Jewish. The establishment of the State of Israel after two thousand years beckons a new age of spiritual opportunity for the Jewish people not available before. And now, fifty years after the Holocaust, Judaism is now once again experiencing a spiritual renaissance. It has taken all this time for a generation that did not personally experience the Holocaust to be born, mature, and rise to leadership positions. In recent years, there is increased vitality and spirituality among all the branches of Judaism.

2

What Is Jewish Meditation?

Jewish meditation is an ancient tradition. Many Jewish sages claimed to have reached the high spiritual heights that they did through meditation. Jewish meditation illuminates Jewish thought, inspires Jewish practice, and elevates Jewish prayer. I do not believe that a person can taste the holiness of God, the holiness of his own soul, or the joy of serving God without meditation. Most Jews who love their Judaism and their religious practice meditate to some extent, whether they acknowledge it or not. Meditation helps focus our concentration so that we can pray or perform a holy act with the proper intention. For many traditional Jews, Jewish prayer is a meditative experience. Heartfelt prayer often leads to meditative and expanded consciousness. Prayer and meditation are intertwined, like an inhalation and exhalation of the breath. Prayer leads to meditation, and meditation leads to prayer. Though meditation is integral to Jewish prayer, study, and the performance of Jewish ritual, meditation is also a separate spiritual practice in its own right.

What is Jewish meditation, anyway? In its initial stages, Jewish meditation is simply a way to free the mind of all its judgments, fears, doubts, and limiting ideas so that the voice of the soul is heard. In Jewish meditation the mind enters ascending levels of focused awareness, filtering out spurious thoughts that may try to intrude. The Hebrew word *hitbodedut,* used most frequently for meditation, literally means "to be alone." Jewish meditation provides the experience of being alone with God. In lessening the attachment to the physical and extrinsic aspects of self, the spiritual and intrinsic true self of a person becomes dominant and radiant. Jewish meditation, through various techniques such as visualization, mantra, chanting, and contemplation, opens a person to a direct experience of the Divine. This experience is powerful; it is transformational and awesome. It is also ecstatic, real, and holy. A person feels his true identity as a pure divine soul. Freed from the demands of the world and one's ego, a person experiences the sweet yearning and knowledge of divine reality inherent in the soul.

The Bible records numerous prophets and righteous holy people who enjoyed high states of spiritual awareness through meditative practices. There are many references to meditation in the Bible. It is said that the patriarchs Abraham, Isaac, and Jacob, and also Moses, who led the Jewish people out of Egypt, were shepherds because this work allowed them the opportunity to meditate. The Talmud and the Midrash—the teaching of the oral tradition of Judaism—state that over a million people, men and women, were involved in Jewish meditative disciplines before the Common Era. Schools of meditation existed that were led by master prophets under the guidance of the primary prophets, the ones mentioned in the Bible. The early sages were said to meditate one hour before prayer and one hour after prayer, three times a day. They spent six hours in meditation and three hours in prayer each day. No wonder they were on so lofty a plane!

With the threat of dispersion into foreign lands, before the destruction of the Second Temple in around the year 70 C.E., the sages and prophets of the Great Assembly—the chief court of Jewish law—feared that the meditative practices would become corrupted and perverted by contact with pagan meditation practices. They then developed, substituted, and standardized the prayer service that would replace the ritual sacrifices of the Holy Temple, maintain the unity of the Jewish people, and also provide a meditative experience for Jews in exile. This prayer service today is generally practiced in the same form in synagogues throughout the world. Meditation as a separate practice was now closeted and restricted to the elite. Particularly powerful practices like *Maaseh Merkava* (Workings of the Chariot) had additional restrictions, and were passed on only individually to worthy disciples.

With the passing years, the meditative practices of Judaism became hidden and were available to fewer and fewer people. Meditation books were published, but were circulated quietly among the elite scholars, mostly kabbalists. Throughout history there have been periods of Jewish renaissance and renewal when the knowledge of meditation and kabbalah was popular and accessible.

For example, Safed, a city in Israel, was a famous center for Jewish meditation and kabbalah in the sixteenth and seventeenth centuries, attracting to it many great teachers and mystics. For a brief period of time, meditation and kabbalah flourished openly. Rabbi Yosef Karo (1488–1575), the author of the *Shulchan Aruch*, the book codifying Jewish religious behavior, lived in Safed, and was said to meditate and have a *maggid*, a heavenly teacher in meditation. Rabbi Yitzchok Luria (1534–1572), also known as the Arizal (lion of God), lived in Safed and claimed to have received the secrets of creation from the prophet Elijah. Rabbi Hayim Vital, the principal student of the Arizal, wrote a number of kabbalistic books that included practical meditation exercises for achieving identification with God that were provided to him by his teacher. These works were only recently published in Hebrew; they are still not available in English.

In the eighteenth century, a renaissance of Jewish meditation again occurred under the leadership of the Baal Shem Tov, the founder of the Chassidic movement. The Baal Shem Tov belonged to a secret society of meditators until he revealed himself at the age of thirty-six. The lineage of the Baal Shem Tov was passed to the *Maggid* of Mezeritch, whose disciples in turn began Chassidic dynasties of their own that exist even today. Each of these dynasties emphasized different spiritual and meditative practices.

Unfortunately, persecution from outside Judaism and the controversies from within forced the meditation practitioners to withdraw this knowledge from the marketplace. The Baal Shem Tov was twice excommunicated by the religious establishment; many of his successors faced similar opposition. Rabbi Nachman, a grandson of the Baal Shem Tov, had to travel to many communities to escape the ostracism he received from Jewish leaders.

Another holy person very dear to my heart was Rabbi Moses Luzzatto (1707–1746), who was persecuted for his involvement in meditation. Luzzatto, the author of many important Jewish philosophical works such as *The Way of God, The Knowing Heart,* and *The Path of the Just,* was also a teacher of meditation and a kabbalist. He was recognized as an extraordinary genius from childhood, thoroughly knowledgeable in the Bible, Talmud, *halacha* and kabbalah. He even wrote spiritual plays. Though Luzzatto attempted to keep his meditation practice and meditative teaching secret, it was eventually discovered by the religious establishment, and he was ostracized for it. Kabbalah and meditation had been associated with the Shabbatai Tzvi and Jacob Frank, "false messiah" movements in Judaism that had been devastating to the Jewish community. Because the religious establishment feared that Luzzatto would become another false messiah like Shabbatai Tzvi, Luzzatto was prohibited from teaching meditation and kabbalah. Many of his writings on these subjects were destroyed. He was persecuted and constantly forced to keep moving from one community to another. All of this contributed to his untimely death before the age of forty. Luzzatto, together with his family, died in a plague in Israel only one week after arriving there.

The traditional religious establishment has historically opposed the teaching of meditation and kabbalah, particularly to people not steeped in traditional learning. This opposition even exists today. One may still occasionally hear that a person has to be a married man, at least forty years old, and religiously knowledgeable before he can learn kabbalah. I always find these comments strange because most of the leading kabbalists died before the age of forty. Perhaps their early death contributes to some of the traditional fear about kabbalah; however, most of the fear is the belief that meditation and kabbalah will lead a person away from Jewish observance, or that a person will become mentally unbalanced. My experience has assured me that meditation and kabbalah have the opposite results.

Meditation is a door to Judaism for many people; it was so for me and many of my students. Meditation is actually a very powerful outreach tool. Meditation opens people to the direct experience of Divine Presence, which often awakens a desire to attach oneself to Jewish practices and institutions. My students begin to attend synagogue services routinely on Saturdays and Jewish holidays. They take on increased Jewish ritual observance. They light candles. They become kosher or vegetarian. Many choose to learn Hebrew and Jewish philosophy. Judaism is nourishing to them. They want more.

Those people who are already connected to Judaism when they come to Jewish meditation find that meditation also deepens their knowledge and practice of Judaism. Meditation opens them to Judaism in a new and powerful way. Additionally, it gives them the tools to reduce stress and support their personal growth. My classes are attended by Jews of all affiliations, as well as non-Jews. This is very precious. In a time of increasing polarity in the Jewish community, it is beautiful to see everyone sit together and share their inner lives, and experience their love for and connection to the Jewish people.

We don't routinely hear about Jewish meditation and kabbalah in synagogues because it is not yet part of the curriculum of rabbinical training. Sadly, in traditional rabbinical seminaries, spirituality, meditation, and mysticism are not emphasized. Rabbis generally are not groomed to be spiritual leaders and healers, but simply teachers and interpreters of Jewish law. Unfortunately, many rabbis confess to me that once they become pulpit rabbis, their personal prayer life suffers. They feel that they have to be more concerned about the politics of the synagogue than the spiritual needs of their congregation. Rabbis contact me because the members of their congregations are now asking for Jewish meditation and kabbalah. They sense that the prayer life of their congregation will be enhanced by meditation.

Several years ago, I was contacted by a rabbi who wanted to learn meditation. He traveled a great distance to see me. After a few individual sessions, he invited me to do a weekend workshop at his synagogue. I guided meditation into a traditional Saturday-morning service. The entire prayer service was quickly and easily transformed into an ecstatic experience. I intuited that the early sages who wrote the service would have been pleased to see such concentration, such silence, such heartfelt prayers. The rabbi himself was amazed; he had not been aware that three-quarters of his congregation was into Transcendental Meditation (TM). The synagogue happened to be located near one of the main centers of the TM movement. These people knew how to meditate, but they did not know how to connect their ability to meditate with Judaism. Once this connection was made, their Jewish lives were transformed. They were plugged into Judaism. I have subsequently introduced meditation into traditional prayer services at synagogues throughout the country, and have been amazed to witness its effects. Traditional prayers are very powerful if said in meditative consciousness.

God is the essence of Jewish meditation. This is what makes it powerful and challenging. Other forms of meditation, such as mindfulness meditation, may claim to be more neutral because there is no implicit belief in the Divine or concept of a personal God. I do not consider this stance to be a neutral position. It is as much an expression of ideology as is theistic ideology. Whether God is in the meditation is a very important difference. There is no such thing as being neutral or value-free. Your religious ideology, or lack of one, as well as the religious ideology of the meditation practice, will shape, enhance, and alter your interpretation of the meditation experiences you have.

Mindfulness and other generic meditation or stress reduction techniques have been accepted increasingly in the professional community. More and more mental health professionals utilize meditation as a treatment modality because of its effectiveness in reducing anxiety and facilitating positive changes in a person. In my work as a psychotherapist in a psychiatric clinic, I also use generic or transpersonal meditation. When appropriate, I even tailor the meditation to the spiritual and religious belief system of the client. I draw on a variety of generic resources in my teaching of meditation as well. My work in meditation has been influenced by my having been a Hatha Yoga teacher, a holistic health counselor, and a clinical social worker. The initial meditation exercises in this book are generic; they are not particularly Jewish. I use these generic techniques as a foundation of skill training, not as an end in themselves. This is one important difference.

People who have done extensive Eastern meditation practices may face certain challenges when beginning Jewish meditation. Comparing one path to another does not allow a person to be fully engaged in either path; it's like being with one man and having images of another one come to mind at the same time. This is a handicap faced by many who have had spiritual experiences in other paths. Let's face it: We're not spiritual virgins. What we have experienced previously in other paths affects our current experience in Judaism. We are not a blank slate. If we have invested much time and effort in a particular meditative discipline, it is often hard to relinquish it for another. On the other hand, we are not spiritual novices either. We have been awakened and expanded by our spiritual experiences outside of Judaism. Because of this, we need our Judaism to be something equally deep and strong.

For example, I have recently begun to work with a woman who spent five years living in Japan studying Buddhism, and who is presently working on her dissertation on some exotic aspect of Buddhism. She can't help but bring Buddhist symbols into her meditations and reflect on the presented ideas from a Buddhist perspective. While I am guiding meditation with visual images of the Holy Temple or Hebrew letters, she can't help but contemplate the inner nature of Buddha and see mandalas and lotuses. It is a little frustrating for her, yet it's natural that she does this, because Buddhism has become a part of who she is. It has penetrated her subconscious mind. This also happened to me when I first began in Judaism. Just as I did, however, if she chooses Judaism to be her spiritual path, she will have to immerse herself with the kind of depth and dedication she gave to her study in Buddhism. Only then will she begin to truly experience Jewish meditation.

Your willingness to be open, to be a beginner, is your greatest asset in meditation. The Bible starts with the phrase "In the beginning" to teach us that we are all beginners in life. Every moment is a new beginning, a new creation. That is why I can teach the same meditations over and over, and it is always exciting to me. My experience is always new. What I experienced yesterday is different from what I will experience today. I have found that repetition creates not boredom, but depth. If you hold this awareness in meditation and generally in your life, you will be open to greater depth. There is always more and there is always deeper. Remember that wherever you are in your life, this is where you begin. Accept where you are and know that it is from here that you begin. We complete and master one lesson in life, only to be given another challenge and another opportunity to begin anew.

You will find that as you repeat the meditations in this book your meditation experiences will deepen. Of course, there will be times of resistance, obstacles, and challenge along the way, but do not let that discourage you. It is a test. We are all tested in life. Know at the onset that this work is challenging. Sometimes even a person who loves to meditate experiences fear and resistance. Resistance is inherent in any spiritual practice because our ego and our worldly self may be threatened by our involvement in spirituality. Take note of what the challenge that comes up for you means to you, and welcome the opportunity it offers you to grow. Remember that the benefits of meditating will outweigh any discomfort you may have in actually meditating. Your commitment to meditation will transform any challenge into a spiritual opportunity. More important, you will be better able to handle and transform the challenges in your personal life because of the time you spend meditating.

No one in Judaism promises "God realization" if you meditate for so many years as you may hear advertised in other meditation traditions. There is a reluctance among Jewish spiritual teachers to describe spiritual experiences or attainment. Such things are hidden. We find few recorded testimonies. No one in Judaism ever says that they have spiritually "arrived," that they have complete knowledge of God. It is impossible. God is infinite, and the path to God is infinite. The more we know in Judaism, the more we realize that we do not know, and the humbler we become. Moses, the greatest Jewish prophet, was said to be the most humble person. In Judaism, we all begin and end as seekers. It is not in our capability as human beings to fully reach Godhood, as we are limited by our physicality, by our humanity. Unlike other traditions, the highest people in Judaism are considered holy, but never perfect.

3

Meditation Guidelines
and Instructions

You may undertake this program as a solitary adventure or with a small group of friends. The optimal size of such a group is between two to ten people, to encourage an atmosphere of spiritual intimacy. Sharing this work will support your growth in a way that will be different from what it would have been had you done this work alone. It will be easier to do the meditations as you take turns reading the meditation instructions. Remember to read the instructions slowly, giving people adequate time to follow the instructions. Even if you are the person to read the instructions aloud, you can follow them as well. When you meditate with other people, your meditations are deeper. You are able to discuss and digest important ideas together, share your meditation experiences, and do the accompanying psychospiritual exercises. Each person should have a copy of this book, as well as a personal journal. Even if you do this work with a group, it is also important that you practice on your own.

If you do meditate in a group, know that you will be encouraged to share your innermost self with others in a way that initially may be uncomfortable and new for you. As much as we human beings want intimacy with others, we may fear revealing ourselves. In our daily lives, we seldom have the opportunity to share our inner lives with our loved ones, much less with people we barely know. I have seen through my teaching experience that people who are most resistant to this kind of sharing tend to benefit the most from it. The sharing exercises will enrich your experience in Jewish meditation.

In convening a Jewish meditation group, you may want to use someone's home as the meeting place. Judaism has always emphasized that the home is the spiritual center of a person's life. In our busy modern life, we sometimes forget this. For some of us, it is important to be reminded that our prayer life is not confined to the time we spend in a synagogue. Too often, we compartmentalize our lives. We feel that there is our work life, our family and relationship life, and then there is our spiritual life. We view these aspects of our life as separate from each other. This is not true. We have one life and there is one God. A father brought his eleven-year-old daughter to a meditation class I was conducting. As she did not speak during sharing at the conclusion of the class, I asked her after class what she had experienced. She succinctly summed up the essence and goal of my work in Jewish meditation: She had learned that God is not just in the synagogue, but with her at all times.

Convening a meditation group in a synagogue may be preferable in certain situations. A meditation group is an excellent outreach program for a synagogue. It will attract new people. So many have been turned off by the materialism, dogma, and lack of spirituality they experienced in their contacts with Judaism; they may feel that Judaism as a religion and as a community is not concerned about their welfare and personal transformation. Having a nurturing experience at a synagogue may help them open to the more traditional aspects of Jewish life.

Ultimately the place is less important than the space. Wherever the group meets, it is most important that there be no interruptions during the time of the meetings. The space should be quiet and clean, with comfortable chairs, and pillows for people who want to sit on the floor. People should sit in whatever seat is most comfortable for them. There is no advantage to sitting on the floor, particularly if you are not going to be comfortable sustaining this posture for the duration of the meditation. The use of candles is recommended, as it creates an atmosphere conducive to meditation.

Anyone from the age of thirteen should participate in this Jewish meditation program. Younger children may also participate, if they are so inclined. My teaching experience has shown that there are children and teenagers who have great spiritual inclination and maturity. The age of the soul does not correspond to the current biological age of a person. People who benefit from this work will continue and be committed to it. Timing is important. A person who is not ready for meditation will drop out, but may resume at another time in life. At the very least, exposure to Jewish meditation plants seeds in a person's consciousness that often bear fruit later.

The meditations and exercises in the book should be done at your own pace. Though each chapter builds on the material of previous chapters, each chapter also stands alone. It is not necessary that you do the meditations in the order they are given to you. It's good to repeat lessons until you feel comfortable, or to return to particular meditations when you wish to do so. Repetition deepens the experience. Please do not let a challenge or difficulty discourage you. Remember that in the areas where you are most challenged, the opportunities for growth are the greatest. Do not judge yourself harshly if you have difficulty with the meditations and exercises. Always be patient, gentle, and compassionate with yourself. Be respectful of the questions you have about the material in this book. Above all, celebrate your commitment to your spiritual growth.

Meditation, like other spiritual practices, thrives on commitment and discipline. Dedication enables a person to overcome resistance and leads to regular periods of practice. With time and practice, your experiences in meditation will deepen.

4

Breathing and Self-Observation

Conscious and proper diaphragmatic breathing is the first thing I offer in my meditation classes and in my private practice. It is the foundation for all forms of meditation, as well as for good health. Breathing is a very powerful tool to relieve stress, release toxins, and vitalize the body and mind. For this reason I give so much attention to it in this book. Medical studies have documented that conscious, slow, deep breathing lowers blood pressure and strengthens the immune system. Deep breathing releases endorphins, natural chemicals in the brain that produce a feeling of well-being and relaxation.

Our life begins and ends with the breath. Breath is so vital to life that we cannot live without it for even a few minutes. Our breathing is usually automatic and involuntary, yet when brought under our conscious control it is a powerful transformational agent. The quality of our life is directly related to the quality of our breathing. Having been told to keep our stomachs in and our chests out since childhood, most people breathe through the chest, shallowly and rapidly. It is no wonder that these people complain of tension, fatigue, and lack of vitality.

As adults, we need to retrain ourselves to breath optimally—from the diaphragm, slowly and deeply. Diaphragmatic breathing, also called natural breathing, is the breathing we did as babies and young children. It is the breathing most people do when they are sleeping. Before we proceed further, take a moment to become conscious of your breathing. Breathe normally. Do not change the kind of breathing you do. Count the number of breaths that occur within one minute, and observe whether you breathe from the belly or from the chest. Let this number of breaths serve as a baseline to measure your progress in meditation. To help you remember and measure your progress, make a notation of the number of breaths you breathed in one minute. You may want to keep track of your breath rate periodically. Over time, you will learn to lengthen your inhalations and exhalations so as to decrease the number of breaths in each minute. To best experience the absorption of a deep meditation, a person will breathe from two to four breaths per minute.

Body posture greatly affects the capacity for breath. Take a moment to become aware of your posture. Is your body open and relaxed? Are you upright or slumped over? Are your shoulders up toward your ears, or are they curved forward? Is your head down or forward? People under stress hold their bodies in such a way that it is almost impossible to take a good, deep breath. Their abdomen is so tight that almost no breath enters there. The chest is concave; the shoulders are often pushed forward, seemingly to protect the heart, so as to limit the breath from fully entering the chest area. The breath is high in the chest. These people take an unusually high number of breaths per minute. The practice of deep breathing slowly changes a person's posture. The shoulders naturally drop, the chest opens, the abdomen softens, the entire body relaxes, the facial grimace vanishes, and the cheeks become rosier. We look healthier, younger, and more vibrant.

Deep breathing promotes physical healing. When deep breathing is combined with visual imagery and meditation, its healing properties are increased. The human body is designed to discharge toxins through breathing. When a person does not breathe optimally, an additional burden is placed on other organs, such as the kidneys, which must work overtime to compensate for deficit breathing. Deep breathing allows for the maximum intake of oxygen and release of carbon dioxide. The blood is reoxygenated. Digestion is aided. Blood pressure is lowered. A person is both energized and relaxed. There are certain breathing techniques designed to maximize the cleansing properties of breathing. Exhaling through the mouth and making a sound of the ocean, making a "ha" sound from deep in the belly, or puckering the lips as if you are blowing out a candle are powerful cleansing breath techniques.

People who are under stress or ill do not breathe optimally. When we are under stress, our breath becomes restricted. The breath is shorter, shallower, and in the chest. It is almost an automatic reflex to hold the breath when we feel pain. This tendency ultimately leads to more stress. Deep breathing helps reduce all kinds of pain. With deep breathing, a person in acute distress or in chronic pain relaxes and loosens the muscles in the area of the pain. Relaxation reduces pain and speeds the healing process by allowing the flow of blood and lymphatic fluid to be normalized.

When the breath is brought down to the belly, the breath becomes longer and deeper, and we automatically feel more relaxed and centered and better able to tolerate pain. As we take longer and deeper breaths, we grow in health. I recently worked with a woman in her late eighties who was suffering from anxiety and tension-related pains in her abdomen that frightened her. Because of the intensity of pain in her stomach, she could barely eat. Deep-breathing, combined with meditation and visual imagery, worked like magic for her. Her stomach pains vanished!

Conscious deep breathing enhances mental concentration and physical performance. Professional singers and actors are trained in diaphragmatic breathing to give them the ability to project their voice. I used to do yoga on a regular basis years ago. By conscious deep breathing, I was able to hold yoga postures longer and do postures that I would not have been able to do otherwise.

There are emotional benefits to deep breathing. During an initial visit with a woman in acute emotional stress in my private practice, I observed her breathing pattern as she spoke about her situation. I wondered how she was able to sustain her life. Her breath was so shallow, so rapid. She was pale and looked ill. Her whole posture indicated a frightened, wounded person. Her posture was slumped over and caved in. Her breathing was high in the chest. I timed the number of breaths in a minute—about twenty-five. She could talk about the stress in her life, but she would have no real relief unless she changed her breathing pattern. I had her lie on the floor and instructed her in abdominal breathing. It was as if she were in labor and I was assisting at the birth of a new person simply by changing her breathing pattern. Breathing from the abdomen was an activity that was very new to her. It was not easy to do this at first. She became aware of tightness, numbness, and heaviness in the body that blocked the flow of breath.

As I instructed her to breathe into these sensations, she became aware of deep feelings of sadness and sorrow that she had been denying. The practice of deep breathing enabled her to access these feelings, and to lovingly accept them and release them. This did not happen in her first attempt, but she succeeded with practice supplemented with meditation and counseling. Through the act of deep breathing and meditation, she has learned how to be present and to take care of herself in a loving new way.

Correct breathing, along with self-observation, is basic to physical, emotional, and spiritual health. I generally begin meditation sessions with five to ten minutes of deep breathing, relaxation, centering, and self-observation. It is not necessary that you do a formal meditation to practice this breathing. You can practice this while you are going about living your life. For example, as you are taking a walk, take a moment to become aware of your breath and do some deep breathing and self-observation. Make it a habit to center yourself with the breath, take a few long deep breaths, and check in with yourself as to how you are feeling. The practice of frequent checking results in relaxation, enhanced self-awareness, and greater physical and emotional well-being. There is nothing particularly Jewish about these techniques, but they are a helpful foundation for Jewish meditation.

The simple and basic introductory meditation practices presented in this chapter assist people in being more fully with themselves as they are in the present moment. We all spend a lot of time and energy worrying about things that may or may not happen. How often do we live in the present moment? The present moment is all we have, yet too often we fill the present with concerns of the past or anxieties about the future. These practices of meditation bring awareness to the here and now. Remember that meditation is not about repressing or avoiding oneself. It is more about accepting and loving, honoring and allowing yourself to be as you are in the present moment.

If it is difficult for you to meditate, please be patient and persevere. This is common for beginners. Don't give up. Meditation becomes easier with practice. You wouldn't expect your first game of tennis to be easy, or that you would play as a professional; similarly, do not have too-high expectations of yourself for meditation. It is common for the mind to wander. Be loving and do not judge yourself harshly if you have difficulty. If your mind is wandering, take note of it and gently bring your focus back to the meditation. If you become anxious or sad during meditation, or become aware of uncomfortable sensations in the body, gently bring your attention to your breathing. Breathe into and through any fear or anxiety the best you can. Meditation is making you aware of your suppressed feelings.

Anxiety is best viewed as a call for greater self-acceptance, compassion, and faith. Meditation will help reduce anxiety by quieting the chatter in the mind and will enhance your listening to hidden messages within the anxiety. It is also possible that you have denied hurt, angry, and sad feelings that now want to be released in meditation. Be open to your feelings. Do not judge yourself harshly for having the feelings you do.

One day, a student reported that she experienced a great deal of anger in her meditation. She shared with the group that she was "actually boiling" with the sensation of anger. This was most unusual, because she was a highly spiritual person accustomed to having blissful meditation experiences, not the kind of person who expressed anger in her personal life. Even in the meditation she had judged herself and thought that she should not be having these feelings. She thought that it was not spiritual to be angry. Objectively, knowing what I knew about her, I felt that she had reason to be angry and hurt about things that had happened in her life. She had experienced a lot of early deprivation in her life, and continued to have a pattern of emotionally unsatisfactory relationships with men. Until this time of meditation, she had not acknowledged or experienced her anger. She was skillful in rationalizing the angry feelings she felt.

I advised this student to suspend judgment of herself, to acknowledge these feelings, to let them flow through her and offer them to God for transmutation. Though anger in Judaism is considered a negative emotion, anger when acknowledged and released in appropriate forum can propel one to make choices in a more positive direction. Anger may enable a person to move away from a negative situation. In the days following the meditation, she found the strength to terminate a relationship with a man who had imposed himself upon her in ways she had not wanted.

If you are aware of tensions and sensations in the body during meditation or in your life at other times, breathe into the sensations. Bodily sensations, such as the presence of tension, may be explored and released in meditation. People often feel tension in parts of the body that relate to the suppression of certain emotions. For example, people feeling tension in the chest usually need to release grief. People feeling tension in the back need to release anger. When the sensations and emotions are acknowledged and experienced, they lessen and dissipate.

Breathe into the feelings you experience, and release them through exhalation. Do not judge yourself. I keep repeating this message throughout this book because we all have received so much contradictory conditioning. We have been told not to feel our feelings. We may feel embarrassed by the feelings we have. All feelings are valid. All feelings have something to say about who you are. All feelings are beautiful, even those "negative" feelings. If meditation uncovers and reveals feelings that you may have previously denied, it means that you are now ready to experience and release these previously disowned feelings. If your body trembles or shakes during meditation, do not be afraid. This is a sign of release. It is safe to be vulnerable. Affirm that you will accept your feelings.

Sometimes people stop meditating when they experience what they consider a "negative" feeling like anger or hurt. This is unfortunate, because meditation is making them aware of what is already within them. Denying or avoiding feelings does not make them go away. Remember that feelings continue to occupy psychic space, whether you are aware of them or not. Through meditation, negative feelings will be transformed and released in the easiest and most painless way, allowing you to open up to greater goodness in your life. Be grateful for any emotional release you experience in meditation. It is a spiritual gift.

Remember that accepting and releasing your feelings does not mean that you have to act on them. For example, feeling your anger does not mean that you have to express it. That is another decision you will have to make. The acknowledgment and release of feeling will, however, enable you to make more conscious appropriate and objective choices for expressing yourself. You will be able to respond to the situation rather than react emotionally.

You may have high spiritual experiences in meditation, wonderful and glorious as they may be; however, if they cannot be integrated into your life, they are only a fleeting intoxication. Judaism is not about escaping to a purely spiritual world. Judaism is about being present and here in your body, in your life, in this physical world in a holy way. The real and underlying intention of Jewish meditation is to transform your life, to enable you to discover who you really are and what you are supposed to do in life. The goal in your life is to be the best you. No one can do that for you. As Reb Zusya, the enlightened and beloved mystic of the eighteenth century, is quoted as saying, "When I die, I will be asked by the Heavenly Court not why was I not Moses, but why was I not Zusya."

Preparatory Breathing and Self-Observation Meditation

❖ Take a few long, deep inhalations through the nostrils and exhale through the mouth, making a sound like a wave in the ocean. Place one hand on the abdomen and the other hand on the chest. Feel the breath move through the body like an ocean wave. With each inhalation, the abdomen, the rib cage, and the chest expand, and with each exhalation, they contract.... Continue to take deep inhalations and equally deep exhalations. With each inhalation, open to receive greater energy, greater vitality....With each exhalation, release any stress or tension. Exhale through the mouth.... If you like, allow the chin to raise as you inhale, and as you exhale bring the chin to the chest and make a "ha" sound. This will increase the potency of this breathing exercise....

Continue to take deep breaths. Feel free to make any other sounds you like on the exhalation....Really let go with each exhalation....Sound out any tension. Do this for a few minutes and then continue to take deep breaths through the nostrils....Inhale and exhale through the nostrils. Breathe in to the count of ten and exhale to the count of five. Take a few minutes, focus on the breath, and allow the body to relax and the mind to quiet....This quieting of the mind will happen automatically when you focus on the breath. When the mind begins to wander, which it will, gently and without judging bring the focus back to the breath.

Sit quietly for the next five to fifteen minutes for self-observation. Affirm that this time of meditation is a time for you to be with yourself in a loving and nurturing way, a way that says yes to who you are....Becoming aware of where and who you are in the present moment is much like viewing yourself through a psychic camera. Let this be a time of self-acceptance, not of judging, allowing yourself to be as fully present as possible.

Listen to the first question asked in the Torah: "Where are you?" This question continues to resound in the deep recesses of your being. Where are you, [fill in your name]? Imagine that this question is being called out from heaven with great love. You are summoned to be fully present. Continue to follow the breath, pausing in the spaces between the breaths. In the empty quiet space, listen and allow yourself to go deep inside to the core of your being. Go to that place where only you can go. Listen to the voice inside that responds: "Here I am."

Focus on the breath and become aware of the thoughts that emerge from the conscious and unconscious mind....For the next few moments, note the quality and content of these thoughts....Are they mostly future-oriented, about something you have to do or an expectation of some sort? Or are they past-oriented, about something you did or something that happened to you?...Are they judgment-oriented? Are you judging yourself or others?...Is your mind very active?...Are you able to be aware of the present moment?...What kind of thoughts draw you away from being in the moment? Do you have a conversation with yourself when you are not focusing on anything in particular?

As you take note of the thoughts, recognize that you are not your thoughts. Consider your identity as the observer of the thoughts, not the thoughts themselves....Your thoughts simply pass through the mind. You may choose to give more energy to certain thoughts than to others. What kinds of thoughts repeat themselves within you? Make particular note of the content of these thoughts.

Always return to the breath and the practice of simply allowing the thoughts to float through the mind as you focus on the breath. Judaism teaches that we may not be responsible for the thoughts that pass through the mind, but when we dwell on a thought it becomes an expression of self, and that reflects who we are. Note what kinds of thoughts you allow and even encourage to enter your emotional body.

We'll take a few minutes to observe the emotional body. Become aware of how you are feeling right now, without judgment....What are you feeling right now?...Experience your feelings without needing to change, deny, explain, rationalize, or act out....Be with the breath....Be your feelings....This is what you are feeling right now. There is no good feeling, no bad feeling. Refrain from judging or explaining yourself. Just be....Just feel....Now, identify with the aspect of you that observes your feelings rather than being the feelings themselves.

Scan the physical body and become aware of any sensations, tensions, numbness in the body....Imagine that you can direct the breath to those places of holding.... Continue to breathe deeply; breath into the sensations....Now begin to gently open to the feelings that have been buried in the tensions of the body.... To the degree that you feel comfortable, explore the range and depth of feeling that is present for you.... You may recall painful memories. Do not judge yourself.... All feelings are valid and acceptable.... Allow yourself to be present to your feelings in the most loving and compassionate way.

Now give permission to the physical body to totally relax. If you like, you may lie on your back. Feel how each inhalation revitalizes the physical body and how each exhalation further relaxes the physical body. If you are lying on your back, feel the support of the floor and allow yourself to let go. With each breath, allow yourself to relax more and more. There is nothing you need to do right now; just be with the breath and relax with each breath.

Meditate on the inhalation and exhalation for a few more minutes. Imagine you can breathe in to the head to the count of ten and exhale through the heart to the count of five. After you have done this several times, say the name of God, *Yah*, silently to yourself as you inhale and *Ha* on the exhalation. Experience yourself sitting in the presence of silence. Silence is holy. Absorb the silence deeply. What does it say to you? Sit as long as you like and open your eyes when you are ready. ❖

Follow-up Exercises

You may want to take some time to write about your experience in this initial meditation in your journal. What did I observe about myself? How was this initial experience? How do I experience myself in this meditation? In writing about your meditative experience, you may want to note whether your mind was active or quiet during the meditation. You may want to note the nature of any repetitive thoughts or thinking patterns, feelings, or bodily sensations you became aware of or experienced during the meditation. It may be interesting for you to keep track of your experiences.

Follow-up Exercises with Others

If you are meditating with other people, the following dyad exercise is a wonderful opportunity to increase self-awareness and integrate meditation experiences. It also promotes spiritual intimacy among the group members. I feel that opportunities to talk about our inner lives and be truly heard by others are sorely needed. These techniques and experiences are not Jewish, but generic and therapeutic. I call this one a meditative conversation. Consider it to be free psychoanalysis.

Select another person to be your partner for this exercise. One person will speak first, while the other will listen fully. Listening fully is being in a meditative state with your eyes open and listening to another person. This listening is without judgment, and without making gestures to encourage your partner to speak or even to emotionally support your partner. It is the kind of being present and listening that you experience internally in the first meditation, but now your awareness is directed toward your partner.

Too often, in normal conversation, a person listens only partially, preparing his response to what he is hearing as he is listening. In this meditative conversation, the partner is not expected to respond to his partner, so he is free to listen fully. The speaker is also free in a way different from usual. As he does not receive the signs of approval, support, or disapproval present in normal conversation, he is free to express himself as he experiences himself. He does not even have to make sense to his partner. He does not have to explain himself or make himself understood. This kind of sharing is liberating and very beautiful. My experience is that it is precious and holy. It is a practice that you may engage in frequently. I recommend that you give yourself this opportunity several times with people who are familiar with the guidelines previously specified.

In counseling married people, I often instruct them in this kind of sharing. One of them has labeled this experience as "I time." It is a special time when one's feelings and thoughts are fully heard by another. This experience restores intimacy. In this kind of conversation, the tendency to blame the other or defend oneself that often paralyzes couples is eliminated, and is replaced by "I feel" statements. This invariably elicits compassion on the part of the listener.

When listening in this meditative conversation, refrain as much as possible from comparing yourself to your partner or thinking about what you will say when it is your turn to speak. Focus on your breath as you listen to your partner. Direct your gaze to the inner essence of your partner. As the listener, you must keep your eyes open. You may want to offer emotional support to your partner with your eyes, your words, and other gestures. You may feel uncomfortable by not doing so, especially if your partner reveals intimate aspects of self. Know that, by refraining, you offer your partner a unique opportunity to be free to express himself without taking into account your response to what he is saying.

If you are the partner speaking, know that this is the time for you to speak your truth as you experience yourself in the present moment. It is time just for you. It is not important for you to entertain, or even to be understood by, your partner. Feel free to speak from a stream of consciousness, reporting any thoughts, feelings, and sensations that occur within you. Reveal yourself on whatever level you are comfortable with. You may speak with your eyes open or closed. The listening partner asks the speaker, "Please tell me who you are." The speaker speaks for about ten to fifteen minutes. After the sharing, sit with your partner silently with your eyes closed for a minute or two. Focus on your breath.

Then the person who was speaking now asks the question of the person who had previously listened. Ask the same question: "Please tell me who you are." Remember that the sharing is not the time to give advice or support, but to speak of your own experience in the moment. This is a way of sharing with another person very different from normal conversation. If time permits, you can change partners and repeat this exercise with another person.

Practice this kind of meditative conversation only with the initiated. If you experiment with fully listening to people who are uninformed and you do not respond as people usually do, the person who is speaking will most likely feel confused and dismayed that you are not giving him the usual nonverbal and verbal support.

5

Meditation on the Soul and Divine Providence

A person once confided to me that he was afraid to meditate because he did not have a soul. I assured him that he did have a soul, that everyone has a soul. The soul is a gift from God. We are born with it, and we cannot destroy it. We can, however, create barriers that limit our contact with our own souls. It is said in Judaism that when a person does an act in accordance with Divine will, he creates access to his own soul. When he does something negative against himself, others, or God, he separates himself from divine goodness. The root of the Hebrew word for *mitzvah*—a good act, means "to connect."

Some people are more in touch with their soul because they have taken the time to nourish it. People who nourish the soul, who identify and experience themselves as this pure soul, often have a special spiritual radiance. They are happier. Others who live lifestyles in conflict with the pure nature of their own souls may not be in touch with or even aware of this part of self. All the more reason to meditate.

Conscious deep breathing may induce a state of meditation. The Hebrew word for breath, *nishama* and the Hebrew word for soul, *neshima* show the intimate connection between breath and soul. In telling the story of creation, the Bible states that God *breathed* into man a pure soul. Meditation on the breath and meditation on the words "God breathed into the body a pure soul" open our awareness and experience of the connection and dependence on the Divine in the most immediate way. We live and breathe because God wants us to do so. Here is where we start to get Jewish.

The Tanya, the mystical book of Lubavitch Chassidism, provides additional insight into this idea about the breath. When the Bible says, "God breathed into his nostrils the breath of life," the Tanya says that it does so to convey the primary idea that the soul comes from the depths of the Divine. God created everything through speech, but in the creation of man He breathed as well as spoke. The Tanya explains this metaphor further, comparing the difference in the breath that flows when one is speaking to that of forceful breathing. It says: "When speaking, there is embodied within the breath only the smallest amount of the speaker's power and life force, and even that is only of the superficial aspect of the soul that dwells within, but when he blows out forcefully, he blows from deep within himself. That breath embodies the internal power and life force of the vivifying soul." To say that "God breathed into man a pure soul" shows that there is no separation or obstruction between God and man. "For if there were an obstruction, the exhaled breath of the Supreme One would not reach the human body." Breath means that there is a direct connection between the Divine and the soul. Reb Shlomo once said, "Meditation is when it is clear to you that God is closer to you than your own breath."

Though a person often may know himself as the combination of the many roles he plays in relation to others—father, doctor, brother, etc.—Judaism says that the true "I" of a person is his soul. The soul of a person is pure, is holy, and is even considered a part of the

Divine. What a tremendous gift—to be given a holy, pure soul. It is therefore incumbent upon a person to reflect upon and remember as he lives his life that his soul, which is the true essence of his being, is a part of God. He should reflect and ask questions. "What does this Godly soul need? How can I nourish her?" "Am I living a life worthy of a pure soul?" Knowing and nourishing our own soul is the most direct way for us to experience God.

By meditating on the breath and the power within and behind the breath, we realize in the deepest levels of our being that our life is sustained by God. We do not breathe by our own will; God is sustaining our life and everything else in creation. When we truly realize that our life is ultimately in the hands of God, we are automatically filled with awe and love of the Divine. Our birth and our death are a mystery to us. We are born into this world and we will die and leave this world. Our first breath and our last breath, our birth and our death—the two most important life events of our life—are not in our conscious control. It is humbling to realize that we and everything else that exists do so only because it is Divine will. Life is being re-created by God constantly, at every moment. As this is faster than the speed of light, we do not see it happening.

Because our breathing is automatic and involuntary, it is easy to forget about the gift of breath. It's so natural, yet it is still a gift. Unfortunately, when we call something natural, we may take it for granted. Being "natural" doesn't mean that something is any less a miracle than something we call an outright miracle, which is usually something that clearly transcends the laws of nature. We often say that something is natural to imply that it exists independently of God. This is not possible. Nothing exists on its own. Were it not Divine will that everything continue to exist, everything would vanish instantly, leaving no trace.

The Hebrew word *olam*, which means universe, is derived from the same root as the Hebrew word *alam*, which means to be concealed. The creation of our physical world was possible because God contracted and concealed His light. This was necessary, otherwise nothing else but God could exist. To create space for something else to exist, *Ain Sof,* the kabbalistic name used for God, created a void and withdrew His light. God's light then re-entered the void in a lesser and more differentiated expression than what was before. The term *Ain Sof* means "without limit."

According to kabbalah, *Ain Sof* created five worlds. As the worlds unfolded, the contraction became greater, and the light and holiness of God became more encased in garments. Creation is compared to the rings of an onion. What is inner is of a higher level and closer to *Ain Sof.* With the exception of our physical world, the other worlds are spiritual. Our physical world, the last world created, is the most dense and the farthest away from *Ain Sof.* God's light is most concealed in our world, yet it is in our physical world that the divine purpose of creation is realized.

If we want to, we can see a world that seems to run independently of God, or we can see a world full of God. It is our choice. It is also a test. I am reminded of a story about a rabbi whose son was playing the game of hide-and-seek with other children. One time, the boy hid himself and waited to be discovered, only to find after some time that his friends were not even looking for him. He cried to his father, "I hid myself, but no one looked for me." The father reflected that it must be like that with God. "God hides Himself, but very few really look for God."

Life is a game of hide-and-seek between us and God. Sometimes it is not clear whether God is hiding, or we are. Let me share with you an excerpt of a college prayer-poem: "We are hiding God playing the hide and seek game, looking for You, yet afraid of finding You and denying Your existence if we don't. We cover ourselves as Adam did with our own veils of illusions and threads of lies when You call." God calls out to each of us, but are we listening? Many people cry out, "Where is God?" in the midst of suffering, but they do not know how to let God into their lives. God is simply awaiting an invitation.

The Kotzker Rebbe once answered the question "Where is God?" by saying that "God is where you let Him in." This is a good intention to have in every meditation. "Let me open to You, God."

In the following meditation, you will open to the depths of who you are and of your intimate connection to the Creator, Who continually sustains you and everything else. The intention of this meditation is to awaken our consciousness to experience that we are sustained and connected to the Divine in every moment. We have not been abandoned to operate solely on our own. This meditation uses the breath as the instrument for imparting this awareness.

This meditation is particularly good to do each morning. Upon arising in the morning, Jews traditionally say, "Modeh ani lefanecha melech hi v'kayam" (I gratefully thank you, O gracious King, for restoring my soul to me.) Soon after, we say, "O my God, the soul you placed within me is pure; You created it, You fashioned it, You breathed it into me."

Meditation on the Soul

❖ Come to a meditative position by either sitting on a chair or pillow or lying down. Begin by taking long, deep breaths, inhaling through the nostrils and exhaling through the mouth. ...breathing out tension and stress through the exhalation.... Continue to take long, steady inhalations through the nostrils, following the breath inside....Bring the hands in front of you, palms open to the ceiling. As you inhale, allow the hands to float to the ceiling until the hands are extended in the air, palms facing each other....Feel that the fingers are spiritual antennas reaching into heaven....It is a great thing to raise one's hands in prayer and meditation....Feel your desire for heavenly energy....Pause between the inhalation and exhalation.

As you exhale, allow the hands to return toward your lap, palms facing down....This posture expresses your intention to bring this heavenly energy back to earth, and into your life....Feel the hands float with the breath....Pause as long as possible in the space after the exhalation. Be aware of your intention as you do this movement meditation exercise....Do this movement meditation for a few minutes....Some of you will feel energy in your hands, and that is good. Then return the hands to the lap.

We will begin this meditation by chanting Hebrew vowel sounds. According to kabbalah, the vowel sounds connect a person to the soul. As we say each vowel sound, pay attention to where it resonates in the body. Take a deep breath and exhale the *Ah* sound. Take a deep breath and exhale the *Eh*. Take a deep breath and exhale the *Ay*. Take a deep breath and exhale the *Ee*. Take a deep breath and exhale the *Ooh*. Take a deep breath and exhale on the *Oh*.

Continue to take deep breaths through the nostrils... Allow each breath to take you deeper inside....Explore the space between the breaths, that quiet empty space between the breaths, and allow the mind to quiet....Open to receive the incoming breath, and appreciate how the breath fills and enlivens the body and mind....Hold the breath to your comfort level, and then slowly let go of the exhaling breath and feel the release and deepening that occurs on the exhalation....Know that as much as you are consciously breathing, you are being breathed....You do not breathe by your own will, but by Divine Will....Your life depends on God. God is breathing you every moment....Allow yourself to relax and be supported by God....With each breath, continue to let go....You can now relax fully....God supports you. God maintains you at every moment. Enjoy the gift of life in each breath...Feel gratitude for each breath...Every breath is a new breath....Every moment is a new moment....God is with you in every breath....Continue to take deep breaths. With every breath that you take, repeat "God breathes into me a pure soul."

Be absorbed in the act of breathing. When the mind begins to wander, gently bring the focus back to the breath, back to the present moment. In every moment, with every breath, God breathes into your body a pure soul. This soul is the essence of who you are.

Imagine that God is a glassblower and that your soul is being blown into your body....As you inhale, become aware of God breathing into your physical body the life force or soul energy to enliven the body and make all the organs function. This is the level of soul known as *nefesh*. The seat of *nefesh* is the liver....Take a few breaths and marvel on how all the physical organs of the body function so marvelously....The eyes see and the ears hear because of the soul. What a beautiful, intricate, complex organism this body is. This physical body, your physical body, is a temple for the soul....Meditate on this idea for a few minutes. Repeat the following silently to yourself: "My body is a vessel to house my soul." Or, "My body is a holy temple for the divine soul...."

The body and soul belong to each other, partners for a brief period of time, each enabling the other to expand and to express its full potential. The soul needs the body; that is why the soul enters this physical world. The body is the vehicle for the soul. There are things the soul needs to do that require it to be in this world. The body, on the other hand, needs the soul to elevate and purify it....Affirm to take care of your physical body with the attention and respect due it. Repeat these affirmations with the breath several times.

Now become aware of the heart, and feel God breathing into you a more refined level of soul known as *ruach*. *Ruach*, located in the heart, gives us the capacity to feel, the capacity to feel love, the ability to feel compassion, and strength. The soul loves to feel....Breathe into the heart center and give the heart permission to open and receive the divine breath... Open the heart....Affirm with the breath that your heart is open to receive and radiate the divine energies of love and compassion. Take a few deep breaths.

Now become aware of the head, and feel that God is breathing into you the level of soul of *neshama*, the capacity to think, to perceive Godliness....On the level of *neshama*, the mind can behold the presence of God. Be aware that you are in the presence of God. This is the level of your higher self, the seat of knowing. This is the seat of the witness, the observer.... This is the essential you. This part of you was present in your childhood, in your adult life, in the bad times and in the good times of life.

Now become aware that there is energy surrounding the body. That energy surrounding the body is known as *chaya* and *yehida*. On these levels of soul, you are most connected to the Divine....So expanded, the soul does not fit into the physical body. This is the aura....The level of *chaya* is the level of Divine will and vision....connecting *neshama* to *yehida*. The level of *yehida* is the inner spiritual essence and oneness with the Divine. On this level you are an actual part of the Divine. There is no separation. Affirm that "My soul is a part of God." Repeat this affirmation with the breath a few times.

Experience that your soul is inside and outside of your physical body....Feel your identity as a soul, a pure divine soul, inhabiting and enlivening a physical body....You are this pure soul....As you inhale, feel the divine soul's desire to ascend, to transcend the body, to connect with God. Reflect on the various levels of soul. Climb from *nefesh* to *ruach*, to *neshama*, to *chaya*, to *yehida*.

As you exhale, feel the pure soul returning and entering the body. Travel back in the other direction. Return from *yehida* to *chaya*, to *neshamah*, to *ruach*, to *nefesh*. Rest and internalize on the exhalation. Do this for a few minutes.

To intensify your awareness of the soul, imagine that your body is a candle and the soul is the flame.... Feel that your flame burns brightly.... Alternate between gazing at the candle in front of you and closing your eyes and feeling yourself as a candle.... The various colors in the flame of the candle are said, in kabbalah, to correspond to the levels of the soul.... *Nefesh* is the black light.... *Ruach* is the white light.... *Neshama* is the yellow light surrounding the white light.... *Chaya* is the blue light.... When you gaze at the candlelight, let the light fill your entire vision.... This candlelight is an entrance into the light of the Holy Temple, the light of Shabbos, the light of creation, the light of your own soul. As you gaze at the candlelight, what does it say to you about who God is? What does it say to you about who you are? Listen to the light for a few minutes.

"The soul of man is the candle of God."... Your soul is the flame of God.... Your body is the candle. Your soul is an expression of divinity.... This is not a metaphor, but a description of who you are. The soul is transcendent, rising, flickering, dancing upward. Meditate on this image for a few moments.... Visualize that the light of your soul is shining, illuminating the world. Remember that a little light dispels much darkness.... Your light burns away negativity and impurities within you and outside of you. The more you let go, the brighter the light.

Sit in meditation for the next five to ten minutes. Experience the soul within. Behold the beauty and purity of your own soul.

The Arizal, Rabbi Yitzchok Luria, the great kabbalist, said that the soul comes from a high spiritual world and descends into the body, into the physical world, to raise itself up, to purify, to do good and make rectification for past mistakes. In so doing, the soul can actually go higher than it could had it remained in the purely spiritual world. Being in a physical body is a precious, time-limited opportunity. Remember that the soul is in the body for a very brief period of time in the context of eternity.

Remember also that you do not know the time and the circumstances when you will have to relinquish this body. You cannot take your life for granted. Rabbi Nachman said that every day we need to meditate on the question of whether the life we are living is worthy of who we are.... Take a few deep breaths. Hear these questions being asked of you: "Who am I?" "Am I living a life worthy of who I am?" "What is it that I should do and want in this life?" Let these questions resonate in the deepest levels of your being. Sit with these questions for a few minutes. When you are ready, open your eyes. ❖

Follow-up Exercises

As challenging as it is to face these questions, it is far better to confront these questions at a time in life when one can make changes, rather that at the end of life, when it is too late to do much of anything. The worst horror is to confront these questions on your deathbed and feel that you did not really live your life. You did not do what you could have done in the short time allotted to you. You did not fully live or enjoy your life. The Talmud says that when a person dies and goes to heaven, he appears before the heavenly court and is shown his life as he lived it and the life he could have lived. If the two versions are closely aligned, this is heaven. If they are very different, it is hell.

In appreciation of the finitude of life, reflect on what you want to accomplish with your life. What do you imagine is the mission and purpose of your soul's being in this world? What does your soul need to fulfill its mission, its purpose for being here? What do you want on the deepest level of your being? Listen to the voice of the soul within you. Meditate on these questions and if you like, write about it in your journal.

Dyad Sharing

If you have done this meditation with other people, select a partner, and decide who will go first. In the fashion described in Chapter 1 as meditation conversation, partner no. 2 should ask his partner the following question: "Please tell me who you are, why you are here, and what you want and need," or "Please tell me who [your partner's name] is, why he is here, and what he wants and needs?" Partner no. 1 should respond to the question from the voice of the soul speaking in the first person or in the third person.

This kind of sharing may be challenging. It is hard for us to express our inner essence to others—sometimes even to ourselves. It also is hard for words to capture the depths of the soul. Always feel free to share with your partner on a level you are comfortable with. This is your time. Do not feel that you have to entertain or impress your partner. It goes without saying that all these meditative sharings are precious, sacred, and confidential.

If it is unclear to you what you need to learn in this incarnation or what your life purpose is, review your life and focus on the times and ways in which you have suffered. Suffering is the headquarters for learning. It is a good indication of what you need to learn and fix in this lifetime. We keep repeating lessons until they are mastered.

Some of you may have difficulty doing this exercise because you feel somewhat estranged from yourself. You don't know who you are or why you are here in this world. If that is so, speak about the not knowing. It is okay not to know. Your whole life is for self-discovery. This exercise is an opportunity for you to learn about yourself. Respect your questions.

Knowing that you do not know is the beginning of knowledge. It is worse not to realize that you do not know. If you are in darkness and you know that you are darkness, you will look for light. If you are in darkness and you do not know that it is dark, you will stay in the dark. Reb Shlomo often closed a learning session with the words: "What do we know?" Ultimately, life is a mystery, and our questions are deeper than our answers.

Record the essence of your sharing in your journal. If you are doing this alone, take the time to reflect on the questions and write your response.

Additional Follow-up Meditation
on Divine Providence

❖ Come to a meditative position and become aware of the breath. Take a few deep breaths to center yourself. On a deep inhalation, become aware that this whole world was created by God. Everything is pulsating with Divine energy. On the exhalation, contract your awareness and become aware that you also were created by God. Do this several times.

Reflect and acknowledge that God is the source of your life. You were not born by your choice. Additionally, what happens to you in this life also is not random. Consider that all events of our lives are spiritual opportunities to connect with God. Imagine that everything that happens to you is to bring you closer to God. It's a divine communication. The events that occurred today are messages with teachings underlying them. What are you learning about life and about God in the mundane, daily events of your life? What is the spiritual opportunity in your life right now? How are you being challenged to grow and come closer to God? What is the Divine goodness in what is happening to you? Sit in reflection for as long as you like. ❖

Follow-up Exercise

If you like, take time for writing in your journal, reacting and responding to the questions above or doing a writing meditation. Write the following words in your journal and write from a stream of consciousness:

Now is a time in my life when I _____ *or Today was a day when I* _____.

6

Let There Be Light

Meditation begins with the act of listening to the voice of your own soul, experiencing first-hand what the soul, which is your essential self, truly needs and wants. When we quiet the noise of the mind and open our hearts, we will hear the sweet yearning of the soul for God. This yearning is inherent and natural to the soul. We do not have to manufacture this desire.

Your soul came from a high spiritual world. She yearns to experience the divine light that she knew before entering this physical world, for this is an experience of great happiness, of great love and joy. Though some will say that this experience is reserved for righteous people in the World to Come, the next life, my experience is that through meditation and prayer a person can taste this bliss right now, in this lifetime. The pleasure of this experience is greater than any joy that physical pleasures may bring. This spiritual yearning to return to this place of awareness and connection with the Divine is our deepest desire. It is actually at the root of all our desires for love and joy in the physical world. Unless you have lived a life contrary to the interests of the soul, you will hear the call of the soul for this experience when you quiet the chatter of the mind.

As you give more attention to the soul, the soul feels more comfortable in expressing itself. The soul has its own melodies expressing its love and yearning for the Divine. When you do this meditation, allow yourself to sing a melody (*niggun*, in Hebrew) or two that are beautiful and powerful to you. Singing a spiritual melody, a *niggun*, will amplify the experience of spiritual yearning for you. It will bring you to meditation. Each *niggun* has its own teaching about spiritual yearning. Each *niggun* reveals something unique about God and life. When you sing a *niggun*, listen to it and hear its revelation. What does it have to say to you? What possibilities does it offer you? How does it open you? A *niggun* may be a traditional Jewish melody sung for spiritual experience. If you do not know any such melodies, it is fine to choose a popular meditative melody and sing it over and over.

The longer you sing a *niggun*, the deeper the spiritual experience will be. During a holiday several years ago, at night, members of my synagogue, led by my Reb Shlomo, sang a single *niggun* for several hours. We sang it quickly; we sang it slowly. We sang it loudly; we sang it softly. We sang it over and over and over again. We experienced total ecstasy. We were transported to realms beyond time and space. This kind of repetitive singing, sometimes referred to as chanting, is a most powerful meditation experience. Music can take you to places within yourself that words cannot. Music opens you to your own soul. I often incorporate singing a repetitive melody as part of the meditation. You should do that as well, particularly in the beginning of a Jewish meditation practice.

In the course of each meditation, listen to and honor your own soul's need and desire for God. Know on the inside level of your being that your life depends on God. This is one of the messages your soul will tell you. Ultimately, your life has no meaning or purpose without a connection to God. You must go deep inside to know this yearning as a personal truth. You have to listen to the "still small voice within." If you are sincere, God will respond to you in kind. It has to be from the heart, no lip service. It cannot be perfunctory. Then you will experience a closeness with the Divine, which will make you want God even more. You have to want God with your whole heart. It does not matter how religiously observant you are, how knowledgeable you are, this is a matter of the sincerity of the heart. God wants your heart.

The greater your spiritual yearning, the more you will receive in prayer and meditation. Spiritual yearning in Judaism is not a sign of lack. In the physical world, we consider a lack as not having something we want. In the spiritual world, yearning is actually a measure of the degree of spiritual attainment. The greater the attainment, the greater the spiritual yearning will be. Spiritual yearning is itself a spiritual gift, as it fills the heart with sweetness. The greatest teachers embodied the most intense yearning. Think of the psalms, and all the yearning contained within them.

The famous Kotzker Rebbe of the nineteenth century said, "God lives where we allow Him to enter." We must actively choose to create the opening for God. In meditation, we create the space for God to enter us. We get out of the way. We let go of the concerns of the day, the demands of the ego to receive, and actively choose to welcome and experience God in our most inner being. The Midrash, the Jewish book of oral teachings, quotes God: "Open to Me the size of the eye of a needle and I will open to you the size of a grand ballroom." Though God is not visible to our physical eyes, God is very real and present. God is not a figment of the imagination. Kabbalah refers to this process as "the arousal from below that awakens the arousal from above." Though God does not have needs and desires in the way that we do, Jewish sages and prophets have said repeatedly that whatever steps, whatever opening we make toward God, God responds to us. God "wants" us to open to Him, and assists us in opening. It is important to know and constantly recall that one of the most basic and important teachings of Judaism is that God created this world to bestow the highest goodness. Our spiritual quest for God is not one-sided. As Rabbi Isaac, a great kabbalist of the twelfth century, said, "More than the calf wants to suck, the cow wants to give suck." God wants to give and to bestow goodness. When we open to receive from God, we allow God to give His goodness. This is God's desire. We actually contribute to God's realizing His intention. In this way, we give to God by allowing God to be more present and expressed in our lives.

The word *kabbalah* literally comes from the Hebrew root word that means "to receive." You will receive from meditation what you open up to within yourself. No one can do it for you. You can read about meditation, but unless you experience it directly for yourself, you will never know it. I can describe my experience of eating an orange, but my description will be inadequate. You will know what it is only when you eat an orange yourself. Do not just read this book, but practice the meditations. These meditations are like a great treasure chest, but to gain the riches contained within it you must open yourself.

The following meditation is usually one of the first meditations I teach in my beginning classes. I do so because this powerful meditation imparts basic kabbalistic concepts that deepen your understanding of Judaism. It is a meditation opening you to the experience of basking in divine light. This meditation also provides preliminary skill training to heighten your concentration and visualization skills and give you the meditative tools for healing yourself and others.

Light, in kabbalistic teachings, is a metaphor for the divine influence. God is called in kabbalah *Or Ain Sof* (limitless light). Light has many unusual special properties. Light is the most subtle yet visible matter known to us. The composition of light is most unusual. Light is electric and magnetic. It is both a wave and a particle. Nothing is faster than the speed of light. We see through light, and some of us feel the vibrations of light, but light is not physical in the manner of other things that we see and feel in the world. Light is a visible energy. Though it is subtle, light is powerful. It can transform darkness instantaneously. The nature of light is to radiate. The more it radiates, the brighter it is. Light brings clarity, joy, and vitality. Light is illuminating.

The Bible states that light was the first creation. This light was created before anything else. The sun, the moon, and the stars were created on later days. The light created on the first day refers to spiritual light. Its vibrations are healing and transformational. Spiritual light in Judaism is known as the hidden light, holy light, inner light, original light. Just as the Eskimo has many names for snow, the kabbalist has many names for light. For our purposes here, it does not matter what we call it. Let us be open to experience it first.

People who have experienced spiritual light have a special radiance. Many rebbes were said to be able to see "from one corner of the world to another" with this light. Kabbalists would meditate on this light of the Divine Presence surrounding them and be brought to ecstasy. Spiritual healers generally work with spiritual light to heal people physically and emotionally. This light may be best experienced with our eyes closed, when we are in a prayer or meditative state.

We can understand why the Jewish holidays begin with the lighting of candles: Lights remind us of God and creation in the most direct way. The Talmud says that the holiness of light is that from one candle one can light many candles, yet the original candle still will have light of its own. By giving of itself, light is not diminished. Whenever you light candles, whether it is for meditation, for Shabbos, or for holidays, take time to meditate on the flame of candlelight and view it as a revelation of Godliness. Reflect on the beauty of the light and all the beautiful qualities that light embodies. Quiet your mind and listen. Listen to the light.

"Let There Be Light" Meditation

❖ Follow the instructions of this meditation at a pace that is comfortable for you. Prepare a candle for meditation. Find a comfortable seated position either on the floor with a pillow or on a chair. Allow the back to be straight, the shoulders to be relaxed.... Imagine that there is a string connecting the top of the head to the ceiling. Begin by becoming aware of the breath. Take several long, deep breaths to center yourself and bring your focus to the present moment.... Breathe in through the nose and exhale through the mouth.... Feel that, with each exhalation, you let go of the concerns of the day. Let go of stress and tension. Breathe it out.... As you inhale, feel that you are opening to greater energy, greater well-being. Feel your awareness expand with each breath.

Now continue to take deep breaths through the nostrils, inhaling and exhaling through the nostrils.... Follow the breath inside; feel with each breath you allow yourself to go deeper inside.... Take a moment to pause in the space between the breaths. After a minute or so of deep breathing through the nostrils, reflect on what you would like to receive from this time of meditation.... What do you truly and deeply want? .... What do you want to open up to within yourself? ... What do you want to heal? ... What do you want to let go of?

Your desire and your intention for meditation will shape the kind of meditation you will have. Quiet the mind and listen to the deep desires of the soul.... Consider whether what you want is what you imagine that God would want for you.

Go deep inside and feel your personal desire for love, for truth, for holiness, for God's light, for the hidden light before creation.... Open to the intensity of this yearning.... Gaze at the candlelight.... Alternate between closing your eyes and keeping them open.

Chant a *niggun* as though your life depends on it. It truly does. Express your yearning through the singing. ...Then silently ask that you be worthy to experience the light of the Divine Presence....Ask that you be worthy to experience God's light and love.... "May I be worthy of receiving the light of the Divine Presence?" Repeat this sentence several times.

Now repeat silently to yourself the words *Ye hi or* (Let there be light). These were the first words said by God in the holy Torah. *Ye hi or.* ...Repeat these words as a mantra on the inhalation and exhalation. Say to yourself, "Let there be light" or "Let me experience Your Light, God" or "Let me be worthy to experience the light of Your Presence." If you like, say these words aloud. Now repeat the words *Ye hi or* aloud. When you say *Ye hi,* allow the chin to rise to the ceiling. When you say *or,* bring the chin down to the chest. Repeat as a chant *Ye hi or* or "Let there be light." Feel free to say this both loudly and softly....Allow the expression to come from deep inside. Repeat this chant for a few minutes and then come to silence.

Now visualize a luminous white light entering the body through the head on the inhalation....Visualize that this light permeates the body, spreading to all areas of the body in need of healing, all areas of darkness....This light caresses and heals you on all levels of being—physically, emotionally, and spiritually....Continue to visualize warm, luminous, soothing white light. On the inhalation receive the light. On the exhalation, imagine you can radiate the light. Do this for several minutes.

To intensify your capacity to receive light in your physical body, imagine a symbol like a Jewish star, a Hebrew letter, or any other symbol that has some meaning for you....Visualize this symbol a few inches above the top of the head....Endow it with the power to radiate white light. This symbol also radiates a sense of well-being. The light removes remaining tensions, negativity, and toxicity. It restores health and well-being. We will circulate this symbol through the physical body. Make a conscious note of the areas of the body where it is difficult to do this exercise, and where it is easy. This will provide you with interesting information about yourself.

Begin by visualizing your symbol entering the body at the top of the head.... Place the symbol in the middle of the head. That point is the midpoint between the front and back of the head and between the ears. Allow your consciousness to rest on the symbol. Experience the interior of the head from the vantage point of the symbol. Feel the vast universe inside your own head.... See your symbol radiating its light.

Now imagine the symbol beginning to circulate around the head.... Ride the symbol as it traverses the interior of the head.... The seven passageways to the soul are located in the head. Bring the symbol over to the eyes, visualizing that the symbol radiates its light to this passageway, purifying your power of vision.... Pray that your vision is purified so that you see the good, you see Godliness.

Now bring the symbol to the entrance of the nose and visualize that the symbol's light radiates through the nostrils, purifying your power of smell. Smelling also refers to the power to sense the essence of a situation.... Visualize the symbol going to the mouth, purifying the power of speech. As you visualize the light purifying this passageway, pray that your speech be purified.

Now visualize the symbol traveling to the ears, purifying your hearing. Visualize the light of the symbol radiating through this passageway, and pray that your ears hear only good. The eyes, the ears, the nose, and the mouth are considered the passageways for the soul. The soul empowers these organs, giving us the power of seeing, hearing, smelling, and speaking.

Now visualize that your symbol travels to the neck, that long passageway connecting the head with the rest of the body....Visualize your symbol traveling through this tunnel, radiating light....Imagine that the symbol has the power to remove the obstacles, to take away tensions so as to better permit the flow of soul energy of the head into the rest of the body....Ride your symbol and experience yourself traveling through the neck.

Now see your symbol going to the shoulders, releasing the tension and tightness of these muscles....It is said that we carry the burden of the world on our shoulders. We carry all the "should" messages we have received on the "should-ers."... Continue to take deep breaths to release tensions throughout this exercise....Now float your symbol to the right arm and then down the right arm to the right hand....Ride your symbol and experience your body from its vantage point. Visualize that your symbol radiates throughout your arm....As your symbol travels down the arms, feel that you open your capacity to give.

Now float your symbol up the right arm and then over to the left shoulder....Visualize your symbol traveling down the left arm, radiating its light....Ride your symbol and experience your body from its vantage point....Note the difference between the right arm and hand and the left arm and hand. As you visualize your symbol traveling down the left arm, feel that you open your capacity to receive and contain energy. Now visualize your symbol floating up the left arm and going into the torso.

Ride your symbol in the torso, where so many vital organs of the body are located—the lungs, the heart, the intestines, the liver, the spleen. Visualize that your symbol radiates its light to these organs....Feel that your symbol removes tensions and toxicity. You can even say this silently to yourself....My heart is now receiving light. My heart is opening.   My lungs are receiving light....My kidneys are receiving light. My large intestine is receiving light. Call out and focus on all the organs in the torso. Imagine that the entire torso is filling with white light, purifying and healing all the organs located in the center of your body.

Then bring your symbol to the pelvic and genital area of the body as well as the buttocks....This small condensed and concentrated area in the body. The seat of our sexuality.... The seat of reproduction. The seat of elimination of impurities and toxicity of the body....Visualize your symbol radiating its light in this center of the body....Ride your symbol and experience yourself from the vantage point of your symbol.

Now bring your symbol to the right leg, and visualize that your symbol travels down the leg, radiating light....Ride your symbol and experience yourself from this vantage point.... Then go up the right leg and repeat this exercise on the left leg. Note any difference between the right and left legs.

After you have completed this visualization, let go of the symbol and focus on the body being open.

Now imagine yourself in the Garden of Eden as a totally righteous person basking in the light of the Divine Presence....Breathe in the high vibrations....Accept these vibrations and let them enter into your depths....Let yourself absorb this experience as fully as possible for as long as you like.

From this vantage point of Eden consciousness, look down upon your normal daily life....Behold yourself from this perspective....You may want to reflect on a life situation or aspect of yourself that needs greater clarity or acceptance....If you like, imagine yourself returning to the normal plane of consciousness to feel the constriction you generally experience in your life....Then return to the higher, more expanded level

of consciousness in the Garden of Eden.... With compassion
and respect for yourself, radiate divine light to yourself.... Go
back and forth. This process is called "running and returning."

Now return to the consciousness of being in the Garden of
Eden. You have the power to bless others with this light. Your
capacity to receive Divine light is actually increased when you
share this light with others.... The more you share this holy
light with others, the more you will receive it for yourself. Call
to your inner screen the image of a person you love and/or a
person who needs healing.... Picture this person on your inner
screen. Visualize this person soaking up this experience,
becoming more radiant and happier.... Ask that God's light
continue to surround this person. Repeat this visualization
with other people.

If you like, include in this meditation a person who has been
particularly challenging to you.... This is a powerful way to
transform a difficult relationship. Imagine that God's light
surrounds this situation and this person.... With the breath,
release your negative feelings about the person or situation,
and turn the person and the situation over to God.

If you are meditating with other people, visualize that this
light surrounds the entire group and that each member of your
group is surrounded with Divine Light.... You may invoke the
soul and spirit of loved ones to join this healing circle
now.... See them with you also basking in this light.

Be aware that you are a member of the holy community of
Israel, charged with this mission of channeling Godliness into
this physical world.... You are part of this lineage. This
lineage is thousands of years old. Many righteous people,
many prophets, many holy people who came before now
support you in spirit to carry out this important
work.... Breathe their support into the circle.... Know that
you are also connected to other people on other spiritual paths

who, through prayer and meditation, are similarly dedicated to bringing God's light into this world....Breathe their support into the circle.

The deepest intention of all prayer and meditation is to unify God and the Divine Presence....We do this now by imagining that the light of the Divine Presence permeates the physical world....Pray that God's peace, God's light, and God's presence permeate the town or city in which you live. Imagine that you can now direct God's light to your city, and visualize that the inhabitants are open to receiving and sharing this light....Focus particularly on the areas of your town where there is despair and violence....Extend this visualization to include your country, seeing God's holy light pervading the entire country....See people happy; see that people have what they need. See people acknowledging God....Pray for the peace of Israel and Jerusalem; visualize God's light and presence filling the Holy Land, and see the people there filled with great joy and love. Conclude this meditation by chanting the word "shalom" with an exhalation several times.

Now bring your attention back to yourself, to your breath. Sit in meditation for as long as you like. ❖

7

Talking to God

Our experience with God is with not just God's immanence and His light, but with His transcendence as well. God is transpersonal. Rabbi Nachman of Breslov, a great Chassidic master of the seventeenth century, advocated the simple and powerful meditative practice of talking to God in one's own words. He said that it was through this practice that he reached great spiritual heights. He recommended that a person spend one hour each day talking to God aloud in his own words. During this time, a person should feel free to pour out his heart to God, to express all his pain, troubles, regrets, needs, and desires, and to ask for whatever he needs to be a better and happier person. He should scream and shout either aloud or silently. After that, a person should try to be joyful. Rabbi Nachman is recognized today as the spiritual leader of thousands of people who follow his teachings and practices even now. Thousands of people engage in this kind of meditation every day for one hour. In Jerusalem, I met people who get up at midnight and board buses that take them into the woods, where they practice this kind of meditation, called *hitbodedut*, which means "to be alone."

Speaking to God aloud in your own words is cathartic and

powerful. Just as God created the world with words, we create much of our life experience through words. A person is distinguished from animals by his ability to communicate in words. Words are very powerful. We can influence others with our speech. We build and destroy through words. We share our ideas and our feelings through words. The more refined our speech, the more powerful it is. When we speak words from the depth of the heart and soul, our speech is most powerful. As the Talmud says: "Words from the heart enter the heart." Our words open the gates to our hearts, to holiness, and to God. Rabbi Nachman says that our speech to God is the vessel that regulates the contraction and flow of God's light. Our speaking to God acts as a regulator, allowing the optimal amount of Divine light to flow to us.

Before we do this meditation of talking to God in our own words, I want to acknowledge and discuss the challenges this meditation may pose to many of you. Talking to an invisible God Whom we cannot see, touch, smell, or hear is a leap of faith. We were educated to believe in what we can physically see, touch, or experience through our other senses. Even though we know that sound waves, magnetic waves, photons, electrons, quarks, and neutrinos are streaming through our bodies all the time, and we constantly rely on so many things beyond the perception of our senses and the capacity of our minds to understand, still we may think that only what our physical senses experience is real. Because we cannot see, touch, or feel God the way we can physical objects, we may question His existence.

In my favorite Jewish classic, *Duties of the Heart*, the author attempts to demonstrate the existence of God by several analogies. In one example, he asks us whether, if ink were poured accidentally onto a blank sheet of paper, we would expect to see legible words on lines, such as those written by a pen. Of course not! Similarly, how can a person assert that the world, which is so complex, so beyond human comprehension, does not have a Creator? Though we may intellectually come to accept that God exists, it is yet another thing to believe and prove that He cares about His creation. This entire book is devoted to helping us understand the love of God and what it means to trust and love God.

Let's be honest. It is important to acknowledge that most of us have some ambivalence and confusion about God. We struggle with issues of faith and trust regardless of what our spiritual and religious experience has been. Many of us have cried out to God at one time or another and felt that our words did not make a difference. We need not delve too deeply into the psyche of most people to find doubts, fear, anger, and lack of faith.

Some of us connect with God only in the good times; others connect with God only when things are bad. Some of us connect regularly. Others do so infrequently. Some of us connect to God in more formal ways by going to synagogue or church. Some of us do so informally by listening to music, being artistic, or being in nature. Very few of us have a constant awareness and connection with God.

I have found that certain kinds of people will say that they do not believe in a personal God. They may say that they believe in God. God may be holy and awesome to them, but God is not personal. God is present, but He is indifferent. For some, God is more like an impersonal energy field, much like the experience of light in the previous meditation. These students may have powerful experiences during the meditation we did in the last chapter, but may struggle with this simple meditation, where they have to talk to God. This is a foreign experience to them. For others, it is very natural.

Meditation is sometimes challenging, because in the experience we have to face ourselves. As much as we say we want God's light, we have resistance. Darkness is familiar to us. We may not feel worthy of being in a personal relationship with God. We may be afraid of letting go of our misery, which we have identified as ourselves. We are afraid of losing the illusion that we control our lives and everything that happens to us. On a subconscious level, we may feel unworthy of being happy. This is true for many people.

Unless we have studied and meditated intensively and have really worked on ourselves, our images of God will be contaminated by our experience of our parents. We carry the images of God that were given to us when we were vulnerable children. For example, some adults who had critical parenting as children may feel that they are not good enough, even though they are externally very successful. I have noted that people who internalized negative beliefs about themselves often project them onto their belief in God.

If I do not feel good about myself, I may not feel worthy of having a relationship with God. Who am I that God should be interested in me? If I grew up with inconsistent and ambivalent caring on the part of my parents and did not experience that they were really there for me, I may experience God as equally absent or unreliable. Because my words and my tears did not make much difference in getting my needs met as a child or even as an adult, I may not believe that they will make much difference to God.

It may be hard to ask for anything from God, or from anyone, when our parents did not inspire this kind of trust. It is a risk. We may be rejected. We may not get what we want, and we wonder what that means about us. Furthermore, to get in touch with our needs makes us aware of our vulnerability. It is difficult to revisit those places of hurt and pain, where we feel an emptiness, and ask for healing.

Take note if some of these thoughts and feelings come up for you during this meditation. Ultimately, in meditation and in life, we have to face our own issues of worthiness. One student shared that this meditation provided rich material for her therapy sessions because she realized that she did not feel entitled to ask God for anything.

A woman came to a class and told me that she could not stay if I mentioned the "G" word—that is, God. She couldn't bear to hear the word. She enjoyed the stress reduction aspects of meditation, but cringed at all the spiritual references. She later confided that she had prayed for her son to live and that God had not answered her prayers. She was angry and wanted nothing more to do with Him. Some of us, like this woman, are so angry with God that we do not want to have much to do with Him.

If you are angry at God, feel free to express it during this meditation. You can be real with God. It is generally hard for me to express my anger to a person, because I am concerned that the expression of my feelings will hurt them or jeopardize our relationship. If you share this tendency, know that this stance is totally unnecessary with God. God can accept and contain all your feelings. Often, when we express our anger to God or to another person, we find that underneath the anger is hurt. If that is your experience, ask God to comfort you.

If, however, we get stuck in our blaming, or, worse yet, terminate a personal relationship with God, we will not be open to receive the support we need. This is a greater tragedy than anything that originally befell us. Instead of running away from God because of difficult life circumstances, run to God, to the One, the Only One who can help you in times of crisis. There is a common saying: "There are no atheists in foxholes." Some of us have to be absolutely desperate to turn to God; we have to be in a corner, in a place of no choice. The anchors in our lives that grounded us, that give us a sense of identity, like our work, our health, our relationships, must be threatened or even taken away. We have to be broken, brought literally or symbolically to our knees through suffering and extreme adversity, to call out to and to find God.

The atheist claims that God is a crutch invented by people who can't cope with the perils of life. This is not true. No one can turn to a God they feel is a pretense or something or someone that they created. If I believe that God is just an extension of myself or a figment of my imagination, I cannot turn to Him when I am in trouble. God is not real for me.

I have heard many stories about people who, in the midst of their suffering, turned to God and found a deep, abiding source of love, compassion, and direction in their life that they did not have before. Because of their suffering, they reached out to God directly from the depths of the heart in a way they had not done before. All the abstract theories and philosophy about the nature of the Divine and reality may be nice, but they offer us nothing when we are in the midst of great pain. At these times, we need a personal God. We need our Divine Father, our Divine Mother.

When we truly cry out to God and make ourselves vulnerable in this way, we automatically get in touch with the natural innocence and child like faith God gave to us. We find that God is there waiting for us all the time. As Jews say every day in the *Ashrei* prayer, "God is close to all who call upon Him, to all who call upon Him in truth."

I often tell this Chassidic story as an introduction to this meditation. It is one of my favorite spiritual stories. In spite of its simplicity, it contains some very important and powerful spiritual teachings.

One day the Baal Shem Tov, the founder of the Chassidic movement, called some of his followers to accompany him on a trip. They boarded his carriage, and soon they found themselves at the doorstep of a very poor innkeeper. When the innkeeper greeted the Baal Shem Tov, he was aware that he was in the presence of a great and holy person. He had not met the Baal Shem Tov previously. He welcomed the Baal Shem Tov into his home and provided generously and joyfully for all his needs as well as those of the Chassidim, the followers of the Baal Shem Tov. To do so, he sold his horse and his goat, and he slaughtered all his chickens. The innkeeper recognized that he had never been in the presence of such a holy person before, and could not do enough for him. The Chassidim were aware that they were imposing on this poor person, but, feeling that they could not say anything to their rebbe (spiritual master), they kept quiet.

The Baal Shem Tov informed the innkeeper of his plans to stay with him for Shabbos and made a long list of food that was needed. He needed twelve loaves of challah, the finest meat, chicken, and fish, the finest wine, and other delicacies. Without blinking, almost as if in a trance, the innkeeper sold his humble home to obtain the money to purchase these items for the Baal Shem Tov and his Chassidim. They had a beautiful Shabbos together.

As soon as Shabbos was over, the Baal Shem Tov boarded his carriage. He shouted to the innkeeper, "I am the Baal Shem Tov of Mezeritch," and he was off. The Chassidim noticed that he did not even say thank you for all the kindness and generosity that the innkeeper had displayed to them.

Sunday morning, the spell lifted, and the innkeeper realized what he had done. How could he tell his wife and his children that they would have no home come Monday afternoon? He was overwhelmed, and went into the forest and began to cry. He cried for all the poverty he had experienced in his life. He poured out his heart to God. He soon heard himself yelling at the top of his voice to God "Make me rich. Make me rich. If I were rich, I would know what to do with the money. I would take care of poor people. Make me rich."

When the innkeeper had no more tears to cry and was gathering himself together, Moshe, the town drunkard, appeared to him in the forest. Every town had such a person as Moshe, who was generally ridiculed and held in low regard by the people. Moshe spoke to the innkeeper and expressed his gratitude for the friendship and respect the innkeeper had always showed him. Because of this, Moshe told him that he was not truly poor but that he had a treasure chest buried in the forest that he wanted the innkeeper to have at his passing. He showed him exactly where it was buried. That night, quite unexpectedly, Moshe took off to the next world.

Early the next morning, the town was talking about the mysterious death of Moshe. Our innkeeper ran immediately into the forest to claim the treasure of riches. He was now a very wealthy man. He kept his promise to take care of poor people, and still he had a great deal of money left. After several months, his wife suggested to him that they go to see the holy man who had visited them before they became wealthy; perhaps he could explain what had happened to them. They boarded their carriage and rode to Mezeritch to find the Baal Shem Tov. They were quickly escorted to the synagogue where the Baal Shem Tov taught, and to his personal study to meet directly with him. The Chassidim recognized them and were a little embarrassed to see the innkeeper and his wife again. They had never understood why their master had acted as he had. But they also noticed that something had changed, that the couple were wearing the clothes of wealthy people.

The innkeeper and his wife were ushered in to see the Baal Shem Tov. The innkeeper said to the Baal Shem Tov, "Before you visited me, I was a very poor man. Now I am a very rich man. What happened?" The Baal Shem Tov, responded, "It was decreed in heaven that you should be rich, but you never asked God for it. I had to eat you out of house and home to get you to the point that you would ask God for what you needed."

We learn in Judaism that a person is created with a variety of needs because this encourages dependence and connection to God. It is therefore appropriate for us to ask God for what we need and want. We need to get in touch with what it is we really want. Nothing is so big or small that we cannot ask God for it. We do not have to reach the point of suffering to call out to God. We can ask God for great things or for simple, basic things like a pair of shoes.

We do so because God wants us to be connected in this way. We are encouraged to ask God for everything and to acknowledge that everything comes from God for our highest good. The Talmud says that the snake in the Garden of Eden was cursed to crawl on his belly and eat the dust of the earth. The curse was not that he would crawl on his belly, but that everything would be available to him and he would not have to pray and ask God for his needs. In so doing, God was ridding Himself of the responsibility to care for the snake directly.

It is taught that our matriarchs, (except for Leah) experienced infertility because this caused them to pray to God. They grew through prayer and became worthy of being the mothers of the Jewish people. We also have to consider, when we do not have what we think we need, that God also wants our prayers. He wants us to ask Him and to be clear about why we want what we do.

When we don't have what we think we want or need, it may mean that it is not necessary for us to have it in this lifetime to complete our soul mission. It may also mean that we do not really want what we think we want; we need to become clear about what it is that we really want. Or it may mean that we are not yet the proper vessels to receive what we want. We may need to reflect on how we can open and grow to become worthy of the additional blessings we want in our life.

Jewish teachings assure us that though God may not always respond to our requests in the time and the way we want, our prayers are heard. Our prayers, our words, do make a difference. Some prayers are more effective than others. Words that are spoken from the heart are heard more than words spoken in a rote manner. Just as we respond more to the words people speak in sincerity, so does God.

It is important to note a spiritual principle in the story I told earlier that may not have been obvious. The innkeeper did not pray just for himself; he prayed that he should have money so that he would be able to take care of poor people as well as his own family. He entered into a partnership with God. He transcended his personal needs and became a greater person. In doing this, he was worthy of receiving greater blessings. When we request what we need to be a partner with God, what we need to enable us to better serve God and His will, God has an interest in answering our prayers. These kinds of prayers have a greater likelihood of being favorably answered than prayers that are solely for one's personal benefit. A person who frames his personal requests in this way is a larger, more worthy human being with a greater capacity to both give and receive.

A few years ago I was quite ill. One night, after receiving very strong medication without being informed of its possible side effects, I experienced a health crisis. When I called the doctor, I discovered that his emergency telephone number was out of order. I did not know what to do. I was frightened. With what little energy I could muster, I prayed to God for relief and for my life. I told God that I wanted to live; if He granted me this privilege, I would write a book on Jewish meditation as soon as possible. I made a deal with God. I knew that God would want this book to be written, for it would inspire others to come close to Him.

Actually, I had wanted to write this book for many years, but had procrastinated with many excuses. I thought that I could not write a book unless I was living in the country and writing a book was all that I would do. I never found the country home or the time when I would be free just to write. One thing you learn when you are seriously ill is that there is no time to delay doing and saying what is important. Thank God, I recovered from the illness. Much to my surprise, when I was beginning to feel better, just as I was cleaning my house for Passover and getting my life back in order, I received a call from a freelance literary agent looking for clients. She had just become aware that I taught Jewish meditation and thought that Jewish meditation would be a good subject for a book. This was my sign from God. It was time to begin this project.

Though this agent did not like my writing style and rejected me, I found a very established and greatly respected agent from a well-known agency who believed in me and this project. Within a month or so, the agent found me a contract for this book. Everything about this book has come so easily. God truly has been my partner. Interestingly enough, I initially submitted the proposal for this book on Chanukah. I had to rewrite and resubmit it, which I did by Tu B'Shvat. I got an oral commitment for a book contract right before Purim, and the written papers came right before Passover. I completed the first draft of the book right before Rosh Hashanah. And I did all of this with a full and busy work schedule.

Another Chassidic story illustrates this point, as well. A wealthy man was asked what the source of his wealth was. He said that his partner was responsible for his success. When asked to identify his partner, he said that it was God. In telling his story, he recounted how he had been threatened by bankruptcy. In the anguish of poverty and pending ruin, he cried out to God for help. It then occurred to him that he needed a partner to help him in the business. He decided that God would be the best partner. He conferred with God every day and shared his profits with Him, and the business had thrived since then. Incidentally, it is a well-known Jewish teaching that the way to receive the blessings of wealth and health is to give charity.

When you do the following meditation, begin by reflecting on what you want and need in your life. Ask that you become a better person, more worthy of greater blessing and goodness. What inside you needs fixing? What is the pain you feel inside? Confess to God the ways you acted that were not in accordance with your highest good. Express your regret for the ways in which you may have hurt others or yourself. Speak of the good points that are within you, and how you need His help to refine and purify your character. Listen to and speak of the deeper desire of your soul to be close to the Creator. Speak to God about the yearning to be close to Him. Speak to God to help you develop greater faith and trust in Him.

If you feel a need in your life for material or emotional blessings, reflect on whether you need them for your spiritual growth. Material and emotional requests are best asked for as a means to support your spiritual growth and your ability to serve God and God's creation. Material things in themselves are empty and meaningless, and possibly may even be harmful to your well-being. It is best to ask for what you want, but with the stipulation that it be given to you only if it is for your highest good. Contact the deep desire within you to align your personal will with Divine will, to want what the Divine wants for you.

When we ask God repeatedly for something too specific, we may get it, but it may not be the best thing for us. For example, a female student recently met a man she was attracted to and wanted to date. She wondered whether it was appropriate for her to ask God for this man. I advised her to not pray for this specific man's attention because he might not be the right man for her and God might answer her prayers. It is, however, appropriate for her to pray for her soulmate, to remind God that the Torah says that it is not good for a person to be alone. She should reflect on how finding her soulmate would make her a better person and help her in her service to God.

Work may be a big concern in your life, as it is for many people. Speak to God about the struggles you may be having in finding the proper work. Ask for work that enables you to come close to God. Ask for money because having money and a good livelihood gives you more time for spiritual learning and practice. It enables you to take better care of yourself and others, and enables you to give charity to those in need. This kind of request is not for one's self alone, but is a deeper request to help bring Godliness into this world. Remember that requests that are in accordance with the Divine will and purpose of creation are better received and honored. Generally, when a person opens to what the Divine wants to give, he will receive more than what he would have asked for on his own.

When you reflect on your own personal pain, go deeper inside and consider the pain and needs of the *Shechinah*, the Divine Presence, which "feels" your pain along with the pain of others. Your pain is not just personal, but is reflective of a greater ontological and cosmic pain. There are holy Jews who awaken each midnight and cry for the destruction of the Holy Temple because God does not have His special, holy dwelling place in this physical world. God is not acknowledged and loved in this world; worse yet, when God is acknowledged, He is sometimes used as a weapon of hate. Imagine the pain of God, so to speak, when He witnesses the senseless suffering people bring upon themselves and others. God created the world to bestow goodness; who is ready to receive? When He tries to comfort us, we make no space for Him to enter and heal us.

Take it upon yourself to pray for the *Shechinah* that dwells among us. Pray that the *Shechinah* be loved and revealed in this world, so that the world is filled with love and joy. Pray for peace. Pray that people be healed from hatred and disease. Ask that God's will be made more clear to you, and ask what role you may play in bringing greater unification between God and the *Shechinah*. Pray that you be empowered and supported to do what you can do.

One of my students revealed a most amazing experience in feeling the pain of the *Shechinah*. This student, a young man in his early twenties, had been heartbroken about a recent rejection by a woman he had loved. In the midst of his tears over his loss, he soon found himself crying for God, Who wants people to love each other but they all too often fail to do so. He felt God's pain, and cried more deeply. A few days later, "out of the blue," he was invited to go to California. Once there, he felt better. One day while he was alone, he had a spontaneous meditation experience where he was filled with the love of God and a sense of the oneness with all of creation. It was an ecstatic experience. God comforted him and gave him this spiritual gift, which has transformed his life.

This meditation is an opportunity to talk to and be heard by the One Who knows you, the One Who created you. If this meditation poses particular challenges to you because you do not believe in a personal God, experiment with yourself now and pretend that you do for the purposes of this meditation. Feel free to talk to God about why you do not believe in God. Give yourself permission to be real with God.

It is the practice of the Staliner Chassidim to yell and scream to God in the loudest voice possible. You can hear them praying blocks away. I have heard people do this meditation yelling, screaming, crying, and laughing as they release very deep feelings. It has even happened in my classes. Reb Shlomo, however, recommended that we speak to God softly. He said that this is the most powerful and the most holy way. When a person whispers, it is like a holy wind rising from the depth of the soul. We tell our secrets in a low voice. Lovers whisper to each other. There is actually more fire in your words when you talk softly. When I teach this meditation, most often people speak softly to God. It is so sweet and so intimate. It is awesome!

"Talking to God" Meditation

❖ Take a few deep breaths to relax the mind and the body. Imagine that you will have the opportunity to talk directly to the Creator of the Universe. Take a few minutes to prepare for this meeting....Begin by getting in touch with what you are feeling right now....What would you like to say to God? Reflect on what you want in your life....What do you want to express more fully?....What do you want to let go of?... What do you want from God?....What do you want to give?

Set your timer for fifteen minutes. Take a few deep breaths....For this meditation you may either stand, sit, kneel, or prostrate yourself on the floor. Imagine that God is in front of you....Feel free to conceive of God in any way that makes you comfortable....Open to the opportunity of speaking directly to God in your own words....Enter into a conversation with God....Open to the possibility that your words are indeed heard by God and that they do make a difference. God is your Creator and is responsible for your being on this earth in the manner you are.

Though God is awesome, God is not remote....God is very close to you....God is with you now....You can say anything to God....You can ask for anything....God wants to be in relationship with you. God wants to bestow goodness and grace upon you....Ask Him for what you want and need.... Tell God why and how it will make you a better person....Ask Him to help you fulfill your purpose for being here on earth....Ask Him to bring you to a deeper awareness of His presence....Ask to be brought closer to God.

Talk to God as if He were your best friend....Tell God about what is happening in your life, your challenges, your hardships, and your joys....Share with God all your pain.... Cry to Him....God is truly your best friend....God is the friend who never leaves you. God has been with you from before you were born, remains with you throughout your life, and will be with you when you leave this world....God is there for you in the good times and in the hard times....God knows who you really are and loves you with an everlasting love. As your Creator, God knows what you really need. With great love, God patiently waits to hear from you. Ask God to enter your life....Ask God for the healing and the comfort you need....In addition to praying for your own needs, consider the needs of your friends and family, and ask God to help them as well.

If it is hard for you to talk to God in this way and feel God's presence before you, ask God to help you. Plead and beg if necessary....Tell God how important it is to you to be connected....Tell God that your life has no meaning if you do not experience your connection to Him.

If you feel that you have suffered unfairly in your life and you are angry at God, it is okay to express your anger. You can be real with God. To have a real relationship with God, you must be willing to be real

Take time to listen to the responses that occur within you. Periodically take deep breaths....Be still and listen... Remember, as it says in the Bible, God is heard in the "still, small voice" within you. Quiet the mind; stop talking; be silent. Create the space inside to listen to God's response to you....Listen....Allow God to reveal Himself to you.

(Give yourself a minimum of fifteen minutes to do this meditation. If you or others want more time, it is fine to take additional time.)

You are in the presence of God. Now, become aware that foremost you are a child of God....You were created for love, through love, and because of love. Open to the experience of being loved unconditionally, as a parent loves a newborn baby....Hear the words of the prophet Isaiah: "I have loved you with an everlasting love." God speaks these words to you!...You are God's child....Soak in this experience for a few minutes.

Now imagine yourself as a servant of God, ready to do God's work, to bring more Godliness into this world in the unique way only you can do. You are here because you have something unique to give....God is empowering you to do what you need to do on this earth....Deep inside, you have a great desire to serve God and His creation. Be with this experience for a few minutes and listen to any insights about what your particular contribution is....There is something in this world that only you can do. Don't belittle what you do....What we think are very small actions may move heaven and earth.

Allow the love for God to intensify, and imagine that you are a lover of God, longing and yearning for the experience of intimacy with the beloved....If you like, place your hands around your body as if you are giving yourself a hug. Imagine that you are being embraced by God....Take a few deep breaths to breathe in the love. This is the sweetest, most intimate connection you may have with God....You are the beloved of God....God is your beloved. In the prophecy of Hosea, God says: "I do not want to be your master, but your husband." God is the true beloved....This is the greatest joy and the highest experience. "I am my beloved and my beloved is mine." This is union. This is oneness. This is the Holy of Holies. This is the highest state. Open to the ecstasy of being close to the Divine in this way. ❖

Follow-up Exercises

Do this meditation many times. Each time you do this meditation, choose two of the following exercises.

1. *Keep a Journal:*

   a. Write to God in your own words in your journal. This is a spiritual practice I began in college when I was alienated from religious life. I always share this practice with my beginning students, and have assembled many extremely moving letters. (I have decided to collect these letters, so if you would like to share your letter to God, which possibly may be printed in a book, please forward a copy of your letter to me.)

   b. Take a few moments to center yourself and imagine how God sees you and what God would say to you. Seeing yourself through the eyes of God, write a stream-of-consciousness letter, beginning, "This is what I want to say to you...."

2. *Sharing:* If you are doing this meditation with other people, take turns sharing with each other what your experience was in

talking to God. If you like, read to each other the letters to God and from God that you have each written. Please overcome your shyness. We can easily inspire and touch others deeply when we share our heart and soul. Honor whatever you have written even if your letter is full of questions.

I recently witnessed a powerful example of this kind of sharing. A few weeks ago, I was teaching this meditation to teenagers at a Hebrew school. One boy gave me the first impression that he was a macho kind of guy, a little bit of a rebel. He made me a little nervous because he was making faces through part of my presentation. During the break, all the girls were hanging around him, with those starry eyes girls sometimes have. After the break, I guided the class in the experience of talking to God, and followed by everyone's writing a letter to God. I assembled the group at the end and asked whether anyone would be willing to share. I was very surprised when this boy chose to read his letter to God. It was so soulful, so questioning, so filled with deep feelings, that he actually cried as he read the letter. His sharing helped bring the class to a spiritually intimate and special moment. The teachers had no idea that he held such feelings and was a person of such depth. He had done a good job in hiding that part of himself.

3. *Dyad Sharing:* Speak again with a partner, as you have done in the previous meditations. Following the same instructions as described in previous chapters, ask the question: "Please tell me who [the name of the person] is. What does she need or want?" Answer the question in the third person. Reb Zusya never referred to himself in the first person. He believed that there was only one "I" in the world, that is, the "I" of God. Zusya would always say, "Zusya wants, Zusya thinks," etc. If you have a Jewish name, it would be preferable for you to use it. You may feel awkward at first, but it is very interesting to experience and speak of yourself in the third person. If doing this proves too much for you, it is fine to respond naturally to the question. Each partner should speak for ten to fifteen minutes. I

have experimented in talking to God in the third person, and have
found it to be liberating. You may want to try it as well.

4. *Praying for Others:* Tell a person in the group what you prayed
to God for. Ask him or the group to pray for you. If the group
prefers, each person should write down on a piece of paper a few
things that he wants to be prayed for by a member of the group. Each
person signs his name to the piece of paper, and all the papers are put
together. Each person should select a piece of paper with written
requests. It is preferable that you do not reveal your identity to the
person you will keep in your prayers. Affirm that you will include
this person's requests in your meditations and prayers.

One student expressed concern that meditating and praying for
others would deplete her spiritually. This is a common concern.
People think that there are only so many things they can ask of God,
and that they may use up their own accounts by praying for others.
This is not true. In the physical world, when I give something away, I
do not have it. In the spiritual world, when I give something away,
the more I have it. The more I pray for others, the more I bless
others, the more I meditate for God's sake, the more I receive for
myself. I become a conduit, a partner with God. Remember that
God is an infinite well of blessing. This well does not dry up.

When you pray for others or even for yourself, begin by
recognizing and acknowledging that God is the most powerful
source of compassion and blessing. It goes without saying that God
wants people to receive the highest goodness they are able to attain.
Ask God to shine His light and give forth His blessing to the person
you are praying for. Visualize the person you are praying for is
receiving God's light and blessings. See the people opening to
receive the particular blessings they have requested. Visualize them
surrounded by white light. Thank God for hearing your prayer and
responding to your request. I promise you that you will feel quite
differently when you come before God requesting the needs of

others as well as your own After a month or so, reveal your identity to your prayer buddy.

According to medical studies, prayer does make a difference. I recommend that you read Dr. Larry Dossey's books *Healing Words* and *Prayer Is Good Medicine* for detailed information about the scientific investigation into the healing power of prayer. He cites one study where heart patients were divided into two groups. One group was prayed for, the other was not. Neither group was aware of the study. The group that was prayed for recuperated significantly quicker.

5. *Expanding Your Prayers:* Make a prayer list of people you know who need to be healed, to get married, to have children, to earn money. Without much effort, you'll soon have a long list of people. I generally ask people whether they would like me to pray for them. Inevitably they are happy and grateful to be prayed for. Sometimes, however, a person is private, or does not want to acknowledge that he has a particular need. If I feel concerned about such a person, I will pray for him as well—without telling him, because I do not want to embarrass him. When people are aware that I pray for people, they call me up to ask me to pray for them or for their loved ones. Sometimes I ask people to pray for me. If you want, let people know that you are willing to include other people in your prayers and ask others to pray for you.

I know someone who has taken on the practice of praying for the healing of others. For two to three hours each day, he recites psalms and reads a list of over six hundred names of people in need of healing that he has drawn from the Internet. Interestingly enough, there are more than six hundred people praying for people they will never meet. Isn't this beautiful? I told this man that he inspired me by this practice. He told me that he has received much more than he could ever describe to me. Praying for other people has transformed his life.

He inspired me to take on the practice of praying for my students, clients, and friends during my morning prayers. I find that I feel more entitled to speak to God when I bring the needs and requests of others to God's attention. My prayer experience is actually deeper as a result. I feel closer to the people I pray for, as well.

8

Meditation and Teachings of the Shema

The Shema, the best-known Jewish prayer, is the most profound, and also the least understood. The words of the Shema are as follows: "Hear Israel, the Lord your God, the Lord is One." It is recommended that a Jew say the Shema at least three times a day: in the morning, prior to the day's activities; in the evening, as the day turns to night; and again before the mysterious surrender of sleep.

Most people understand the Shema on its simplest level. The Shema states that there is only one God—as opposed to two, ten, or a thousand. This concept is basic and essential. On the simplest level, the Shema means that there is only one God to whom we direct our prayers. We do not go to one god for one kind of blessing and another god for something else. There is only one God. The buck, so to speak, stops with God.

The Shema, the belief in one God, affirms that everyone, and everything, in creation has the same Creator, this one God. It doesn't matter what a person's religion or race is. We need always to remember that we are all created by the same God, the same awesome, powerful, and unknowable God Who created everything in creation. We all have an equal right to be here. It is God's will that each of us is here. Though we have different parents, different religions and cultural backgrounds, we have the same God. Having the same Divine Parent, we are all brothers and sisters. Reb Shlomo had the custom of calling everyone brother or sister and then the first name of the person. This practice reminds us that we are one family, that we love and are responsible for each other. It is a beautiful meditation to behold and reflect on every person as a brother or sister.

The teachings of the Shema are deeper than all this. When the Shema says that there is one God, it also means that God is unique. If God were not unique, He would be more than one. It also means that God cannot be divided into parts. God is a whole. God is One, a unity. The Bible may say that God is angry, that God is compassionate, but that is our perception and interpretation. God is only God. God is One. Whatever God does is in harmony with Himself.

God cannot be broken into parts, as we can. We human beings have a body and a soul. We have many thoughts, many emotions; there are many parts to us. We exist in the context of time and space. We live in a world of description and definition. We are young. We are old. We are male. We are female. We are ever-changing. We are finite.

God is beyond any description or definition. No words can adequately describe God. Maimonides said that we can talk about God only by stating what He is not. God is not male. God is not female. God is not physical. Most of us do not think of God as physical, but often we think of God as spiritual. This also is not true. God is not spiritual. Physicality and spirituality are equal creations of God. Time and space are also God's creations. We cannot define God by anything but God, because everything else was created by God. A creation is only a part, and cannot be the same as the

Creator. Though creation may reflect divinity, it is not God. Creation is contained within God. We live within God. We are not God. This is an important and basic distinction. As divine as creation is, it can never fully express the essence of God. God is God. Nothing has a reality independent or outside of God, except God.

When, in the Bible, Moses asks God who He is, God responds that "I am that I am," or "I will be what I will be." What does this mean? Basically, it means that God's essence cannot be described or defined by anything else. God is God. God is because God is. He will be what He will be. We need to understand that we cannot understand God. God is an existence like nothing else. God is the underlying true existence. God is actually Being itself. The name of God, *Yud Hay Vav Hey,* comes from the Hebrew word *hovey,* which means "to be." Putting the *yud* in front of the root places the verb into the active or command tense, so *Yud Hay* and *Vav Hey* may be translated as "active Being." When we come close to God, we come close to the underlying reality, the essence of life. That is why it is said in a psalm: "He who clings to God is truly alive." Interestingly enough, Hebrew has no verb "to be" in common usage. For example, in Hebrew, "I am tired " would be "I tired." God is the only Being that says "I am." God is the only true existence.

To relate to God, we form images of Him. It is hard for us not to have any images of God. Yet we have to remember that whatever our images of God may be, they are only our images, not God. It is a pity that we let these images separate us from the experience of oneness with God and from each other. When we relate to God, whatever we may call Him, we must remember that God is unknowable and beyond any concept we may have. God is something else, an other, another dimension. God is infinite and we are finite. God is an unknowable mystery. Kabbalah refers to God as *Ain Sof,* which means "without limit," or *Or Ain Sof* which means "limitless light." In traditional religious circles, God is called *Hashem,* which means "the Name." The Name—what kind of name is this? I can't imagine being more ambiguous about who God is.

Though we cannot know God's essence and how God experiences Himself, we can make inferences about God from observing and studying His creation. We may sense the Divine Presence because God allows Himself to be known in this way. For example, I look at the beautiful sky, see the moon and stars twinkling, and I feel God's presence. I see babies and children smiling and laughing, and I feel God's love and joy being expressed through them. Wherever you look, you can see God's light being expressed if you have the right eyes. There is no place in this world where God is not.

The Shema reflects the highest level of spiritual awareness possible to us. In affirming the oneness of God, the Shema affirms that everything is a manifestation of the Divine. Moses reached the highest state of awareness when he said, "There is nothing but God." The multiplicity of things in the world is only apparent, not real in essence. Underlying everything in this world is the simple unity of the Divine. The *Tanya*, in its chapter *Shaar Hayichud*, (Gate of Unity), explains these ideas by saying that the material world that appears to exist is complete nothingness in relation to God. The Alter Rebbe, the author of the *Tanya*, provides the following illustration to explain this concept. Consider the light of the sun, which illuminates the earth. The light and the radiance of the sun spread a great distance, but this light is absolutely nonexistent in relation to the sun, which is the source of the light. The radiance and the light are part of the sun, and have no existence by themselves. So it is with us: We feel that we have an independent reality if we feel apart from God. If we are close to God, we experience ourselves to be an extension of Him. God is the only true reality.

A spiritually evolved person sees everything as an expression of Godliness. He sees God in the natural order of life. The practice of this awareness will enable us to grow spiritually. It is easier said than done. For a spiritually evolved person, God fills the world, and there is no place devoid of Him. He knows that God is the Creator and the only true reality. Everything else was created by God and flows from God. A spiritually evolved person understands that he does not have an independent existence or reality; he is real to the extent that he is a part of God. His existence flows from God. He aligns his personal will with Divine will. This recognition of his oneness with God and all of creation brings with it the experience of ecstasy.

Meditating on the Shema is our express ticket to the highest awareness of God. What a gift! God told us who God is. "Hear Israel, the Lord your God, the Lord is One." The Shema begins with the word "Hear." This is the call for meditation. Hearing, or listening, is the quieting of the chatter of the mind. Listening is meditation. Through meditation, God is revealed to us. When we say the Shema, we, too, for a few moments may have a glimpse of God's oneness. We feel so happy when we feel at one with one person; imagine the joy at feeling at one with the Creator of the universe!

When I first began learning with Reb Shlomo, he would say, "It is so deep, so deep, there is one God," or "Open your hearts, sweetest friends, God is God. This is mind-blowing." Yes, God is God; that was clear but I really did not understand the depth of his words. What was he so excited about? Was he on drugs? Then one day, while in meditation, I got it. God is God—and I was in ecstasy. This was a moment of tremendous insight that was beyond my normal powers of reasoning or analysis to comprehend. This may happen to you as well. A person may learn many deep concepts about God and life in Torah or kabbalah, but the profundity of these ideas cannot be penetrated or experienced without prayer and meditation. The Alter Rebbe, in the *Tanya*, one of the deepest spiritual books, is constantly instructing his readers to meditate on the ideas he presents.

In these moments of insight, when we experience Godliness, our questions about the meaning and purpose of life are answered. Many times, my students tell me that they experience life in a wholly new and more wonderful way because they have glimpsed the underlying Divine reality of life. Through meditation, they have experienced directly that God is the only true reality; God is the One, the only true One. They then train themselves to be aware of God and to cling to Him. Having tasted the joy of God's oneness and closeness, they feel greater commitment to bringing Godliness into the world. They are more open to see Godliness being revealed in their own lives.

The experience of the Shema inspires us to seek harmony between the physical and spiritual aspects of ourselves. It is important to know that Judaism, with all its commandments, is designed to align the physical aspects of self with the spiritual aspects. When the proper harmony between body and soul is established, we become holy and whole. When we are balanced and whole, we reflect and reveal God's oneness. Similarly, when we marry, love, and become one with another person, we reveal God's oneness. That is why even strangers are happy to hear about people getting married. Each marriage brings greater love and oneness into the world.

Meditating on the Shema and its basic teachings is important because it actually reveals God's oneness to the world. There are many deep kabbalistic secrets about the Shema. For example, when we visualize the letters of the Divine Name, the *Yud Hay Vav Hay,* and say the name *Adonay,* we are actually making a union between two aspects of God. We are uniting God and the *Shechinah.* That is why observant Jews say the Shema at least three times a day. The Shema is central to Judaism.

The Shema is also an affirmation of faith. Saying the Shema brings us faith. Believing in God is a matter of faith. Our tradition and our life experience inform us that there is a God Who is involved in His creation. Though we cannot prove scientifically the existence of God or the divinity of the soul—at least not yet—the true mystic is not interested in scientific proof. There would then be no need for faith. A mystic offers faith as an expression of his joy in and love of God. It is the most precious thing we can give to God. If we were perfect or had complete knowledge of God, or if God were fully revealed, and there was no evil in this world, what need would we have for faith?

Reb Zusya was known to live constantly in the consciousness of the oneness of God. He was very poor, yet was known to say that he had never experienced a bad day in his life. As I said earlier, Zusya always referred to himself in the third person.

Every day Zusya was in the habit of speaking to God and asking for his physical needs to be met. Each morning, he would say to God, "Zusya is hungry." His disciples would hear him and would bring the food to their rebbe. The rebbe would be happy and thank God. He would repeat these words three times a day, and his disciples would hurry to bring Reb Zusya food. Each time he would thank God.

One day, the disciples rebelled and said that it was not God who fed the rebbe, but them. They decided not to feed the rebbe and see what happened. That morning, as usual, Reb Zusya, after the morning prayers, told God that he was hungry. Nothing happened; no food magically appeared. At lunchtime Zusya said to God, "Zusya is *really* hungry." Nothing happened. By dinnertime, Zusya was extremely hungry, and he again said to God, "Zusya is *really, really, really,* hungry."

The disciples were beginning to snicker when there was a knock at the door. A rich man was there, asking whether he could give the rebbe the leftovers of a wedding party he had attended earlier in the day. Of course, Reb Zusya accepted, and really thanked God. The disciples then realized that it was their privilege to help the rebbe, not their obligation. If they chose not to feed the rebbe, the rebbe would be fed in another way.

The Talmud says that a blade of grass does not move without it being the will of God. If you do not have the opportunity and privilege to perform a kindness for a person, then another person will do it. Ultimately, God is the bestower of goodness; we are merely the messengers. We need to thank God when we receive a kindness from others as well as when we are privileged to do a kindness for another. Similarly, when we are hurt by others, we have to see the Divine hand there as well, and ultimately thank God for the growth opportunity provided by these experiences as well.

Reb Zusya was a holy person who enjoyed Divine protection. Yet I derive an important teaching from this story that is relevant to those of us who are less holy than Reb Zusya. If it is God's will that something is supposed to happen, it will. We are asked to trust that God will deliver to us what we need. It is true that we need to do our part, yet the success or failure of what we do comes from God. Understanding and applying these ideas to your life is not simple. It is very delicate. In many cases, for ourselves and others, we cannot say, "Let God take care; I trust in God," and be passive. For example, if we witness suffering, we cannot tell ourselves or the people who are suffering that the suffering is God's will. That would be cruel. Rather, we must ask what we can do to alleviate suffering. It is quite possible that we have been made aware of a person's suffering because we have the potential to alleviate his pain. God gave us an opportunity to do something good for another person. What a privilege! God wants to work through us. We can be God's hands and feet. When we suffer, it may be that we need to learn how to receive from others and ask for help. If we trust that our help comes from God, the people who help us in life are like angels.

It is a paradox. God is running the world; God is responsible. Sometimes, in the Bible, God accepts the responsibility for evil in the world; at other times He blames us. No wonder it is confusing to us. When we consider the suffering in the world, we naturally ask ourselves whether everything indeed comes from God. What is the role of free will in creating personal reality? How can we understand suffering? Should we blame God or ourselves for our suffering?

One of the most important teachings of Judaism is that God created this world to bestow goodness. If God wanted to bestow goodness, couldn't He have done a better job? Rabbi Moses Luzzatto, a fifteenth-century kabbalist, responds to this question most succinctly in his book *The Knowing Heart*. To summarize, he states that though God might have been expected to create man and the entire creation to be perfect in the likeness of His goodness, His wisdom dictated that He restrain Himself and create an imperfect world. Had the Creator created a perfect world, what would man do? Man's existence would be meaningless. He would have nothing to contribute. God honored man by giving him an opportunity to participate in perfecting himself and God's world.

Kabbalah talks about the "bread of shame," namely, the shame and embarrassment that man would experience if he were only a recipient of Divine goodness. If we only received and never gave, we would not feel good about ourselves. We feel better about ourselves when we make a positive contribution, when we feel that we make a difference and what we do has meaning and purpose. When we must overcome our natural tendencies to do something good, we feel even better about ourselves. We value something more when we have worked for it. To give us this sense of independence and self-worth, God conceals Himself from us. With this sense of self, which is also a gift of God, we gain the capacity to make choices.

With the proper thoughts, speech, and actions, we become vessels to receive and reveal greater Godliness in this physical world. In this life we are given the opportunity to become partners and instruments for the Divine. We are not merely recipients. God shares His power with us. When we affirm God's oneness, God works through us. It is said that God feeds the poor and heals the brokenhearted. How does God do this? He does so through us. To be a channel for God in this way is a source of great joy.

Will we make choices that further goodness in the world, or will we make choices that are selfish and separate us from goodness? This is in our hands. With the gift of free will, we become responsible for the choices we make. Our choices affect ourselves, others, and the world. God does not abandon us with this responsibility. In the Bible, God gives us constant instruction in how to behave in this world so as to receive the highest goodness. God is constantly encouraging us to do good and warning us about the consequences of not doing good.

If we open to God, invite Him into our lives, and align our personal will with His will, God will guide us and direct our steps. It is written in Psalms: "God is good to those who trust in Him." If a person truly believes that there is nothing in this world that can do good or bad unless it is God's will, our teachings say, this person will be protected by God. Such a person lives with daily miracles. To the extent that we want to be on our own, God will allow us to be on our own, and unfortunately we have to suffer the consequences. When we suffer, we need to examine our thoughts, speech, and actions because much human suffering is a consequence of our own thinking, speech, and actions. Pain can actually be a blessing from God, a wake-up call, as it informs us that a change is needed. As I said earlier, sometimes we have to realize the absolute bankruptcy of the negative choices we have made and be brought to our knees before we turn to God.

Why people suffer is a deep and challenging question. The kind of suffering people sometimes must endure seems unfair. Did they deserve this? Suffering can challenge our faith. We can view our suffering as an opportunity to grow and become better people, or we can see ourselves as victims with no rhyme or reason. It is our choice. The Shema lets us see the hand of God in even the bad things that happen to us. It gives us strength and insight. I am reminded of a well-known story about Rabbi Akiba. He was traveling one day and wanted to stay at an inn, but there was no room for him. "This must be for the good," he said, and chose to sleep outdoors. He had with him a rooster to wake him in the morning, a donkey to take him to the forest, and a candle to read by. Then a lion killed his donkey, a cat devoured his rooster, and the wind blew out his candle. Again Rabbi Akiba said, "This must be for the good" and he went to sleep. In the morning he learned that a band of wild robbers had come to the inn, looted, and taken everyone captive. Had his donkey neighed, his rooster crowed, or his candle been lit, he would have been discovered and harmed, so he again said, "This must be for the good."

Of course, it is not so easy to see the goodness inherent in our suffering. The Talmud says that God tests the ones He loves. These words have been a comfort for me. I can view my suffering not as a punishment, but as a spiritual opportunity. When we suffer, we often do our greatest learning. Like the olive, which is squeezed for oil, we may become more refined through our suffering. We must remember that when we suffer we do not see the whole picture. If we have faith in God, we believe that good will come from it. We may still be in pain, yet we can accept it with equanimity, believe, and even witness that we have grown through painful experiences in ways we may not have done otherwise. If we do not have faith, we have to ask God for it. If necessary, we should beg God to open our eyes and hearts to see and feel His love and goodness in what we are going through. Meditating on the Shema transforms negativity and gives us faith. In the last generation, we saw that some people who went through the Holocaust had their faith in God destroyed; others came out of it with their faith in God strengthened. Many testify that it was faith in God that enabled them to survive.

The Shema makes available a more complete relationship with God. We experience God as both immanent and transcendent. In this way, I sense God in my most inner being and within all of creation. Yet I know equally well that God transcends this world and is beyond any concept I can have about Him. I affirm both God's immanence and transcendence when I say that God is One. I get a glimpse of the true reality that God is all there is. It helps to understand that we have a different vantage point from God. From our vantage point as physical beings living in time and space, we experience an outside and an inside, as well as a before and an after. God, in relation to God, does not experience an outside and an inside. God is not constrained by the limits of time or space. God is the ultimate existence, and everything flows from Him. God is God. God is One.

Some of us are more comfortable with a God Who is remote, separate from us and all of creation. God is in His place and we are in our place. There is a distance that allows us to breathe and live. God is holy, and we are merely human. Some of us feel the opposite. God is immanent, accessible and available. Sometimes people who accentuate the experience of the immanence of God forget that God is also separate from us. God is also unknowable, awesome, and holy. God is our Creator and we will have to make an accounting to Him. Interestingly enough, in Hebrew, the word holy means "separate." The Shema affirms that God is both transcendent and immanent. God is in everything, yet also outside of everything.

A person can learn a great deal about God through the prayers in the prayerbook. It is a good practice to actually study and meditate on the various ideas that are presented in the prayers. The popular prayer *Adon Olam* articulates these basic ideas about God very clearly. Consider some of the verses. "Master of the universe, Who reigned before any form was created....After all has ceased to be, He, the Awesome One, will reign alone. It is He Who was, He Who is and He Who shall remain, in splendor. He is One—there is no second to compare to Him." These verses refer to the transcendent God. This God is unknowable. This God is very different from me. This song then goes on to talk about God as a personal God. "He is my God....Rock of my pain in time of distress. God is with me and I shall not fear." This God is personal and available to me. I can have a personal relationship with Him. I can see God reflected in everything in this world.

If these ideas about the Shema are incomprehensible and too abstract to you now, please be patient. Some teachers say that we can't really understand God's oneness in this world. These concepts are difficult to understand intellectually as well as emotionally. I have done my best to present some of the deeper concepts that are part of an understanding of the Shema, but I confess that I do not have a complete understanding of the Shema intellectually or emotionally. I am not Reb Zusya. I cannot say that I have never had a bad day. I have had unusual suffering. I still struggle at times to see the goodness or God's hand in the suffering I have endured in my life. I do know, however, from my personal experience that the saying of and meditating on the Shema brings peace and strength. I recommend that you do this meditation many times.

Meditation on the Shema

❖ Assume a comfortable seated position on a chair or a cushion. Focus your attention on the breath. Take a few deep breaths. Breath from the abdomen, to the rib cage, to the chest, and then make a deep, slow exhalation through the mouth, making a sound like an ocean wave. After a few deep centering breaths, listen to this story, which is attributed to the Baal Shem Tov himself.

There was a king who, by magic, one day decided to construct walls and obstacles around his palace to make entry into the palace difficult. He placed wild serpents and lions along the way. He hid himself within the palace. The king then issued proclamations saying that whoever made it through the obstacles and reached the palace would be richly rewarded. Some people tried, but when they encountered the serpents and scorpions at the first gate, they retreated. They were not willing to risk their lives. The king appointed servants to stand behind some of the walls to give riches to those who were able to confront the challenges. Some people found themselves rich and satisfied, but also decided to retreat.

The king had a son who had been separated from him, and who had a great desire to see his father again. His desire and yearning were so great that he was unconcerned about the risks and perils of the journey to his father. When he saw the wild animals, he wept, "Father, please be compassionate, I want so much to see you." His longing was so great that he had no interest in the rewards. He wanted only to be with his father.

When the king heard the cries of his son, and saw his great desire and courage, he removed the obstacles. In a moment they vanished as if they had never existed. The father, the king, was right in front of him. Everything was beautiful and peaceful. The reality of being in the king's presence was so deep that all the obstacles were now seen only as an illusion. He was always in the presence of the king. The obstacles were just a test to see who loved the king.

So it is with us. Like the son in the story, we must feel a strong burning and pure desire to be in the presence of the Divine. This yearning opens our awareness to the reality that we are always in the presence of the king. Yet we must be willing to confront the obstacles and barriers within ourselves. The walls and obstacles that seem to separate God from us, however, are illusory. God is the true reality of our existence. God's glory fills the world. We are always in the presence of God....Wherever we are, God is there. As King David addresses God in a psalm, "If I ascend to the highest heavens, You are there. If I descend to the lowest depths, You are there." There is no place where God is not. Where you are, God is. Take a few breaths, and open to the awareness that God is with you right now.

To intensify your awareness of the Divine Presence, repeat

silently to yourself *baruch* (blessed) on the inhalation, and *atah* (you) on the exhalation. As you inhale and repeat *baruch*, imagine that the top of the head opens to receive blessing. As you exhale, become aware of God's surrounding presence. Repeat this several times, opening to receive blessing. Focus the mind on this mantra.

Now see the letters of the Divine name in front of you: the *Yud*, the *Hay*, the *Vav*, and the final *Hay*. The Divine name is considered so powerful that we are not allowed to pronounce it. Yet, by visualizing the letters of the divine name, we invoke the Divine Presence. King David said in a psalm, "I have placed *Yud Hay Vav*, and *Hay* before me at all times." God is always in front of you. It is a kabbalistic practice to see the letters of God's name before you.

Focus your attention on one letter at a time. Carve out each letter on your inner screen. Visualize the *yud* and seeing the letter before you, allow your consciousness to trace the letter. This is the kabbalistic practice known as riding the letters. Repeat this practice with the *hay*. Now see the *hay* on your inner screen and carve it out. Take a few breaths and now see the *vav*, and carve it out. Take a few deep breaths and then carve out the final *hay*. Behold the entire name of God on your inner screen—the *Yud*, the *Hay*, the *Vav*, and the *Hay*. Seeing the name in this position reflects the transcendence of God.

Now breathe in the *yud*, and visualize it in the head.... Exhale the *hay* and visualize it filling the shoulders and the arms....With a deep inhalation,, breathe in the *vav* and place it in the torso....Exhale the final *hay* and visualize it from the waist to the legs. Repeat this visualization at least *ten* times and then let go of it. Experience yourself as being surrounded and permeated by the Divine Presence. The letters of God's name within the body are the immanence of God.

Imagine yourself in the Holy Temple, that place and time when the Divine Presence was most tangible....Journey back in time....You can access this experience as if you were there. This experience is recorded in the deep recesses of your consciousness. Access this memory. You are sitting in the house of God....As we say in the davening, *"Ashrei yoshev vatecha"* ("Happy are they who sit in Your house"). You are sitting in the house of God. Breathe in this experience and sit quietly for a few minutes, visualizing yourself surrounded by the Divine Presence.

The Shema is the revelation of God's oneness. We will prepare to say the Shema by first working with the letters of the Shema—the *shin,* the *mem,* and the *aleph.* We substitute the *aleph* for the *ayin,* because the *shin,* the *mem,* and the *aleph* are the mother letters of the Hebrew alphabet. According to the kabbalah, the Hebrew letters contain powerful energies. Creation occurred through words, which are composed of letters. If you do not know the Hebrew letters, you can still do this exercise, as we will be visualizing the color and making the sound associated with the letter.

Visualize the *shin* in the head, in orange light....The *shin* represents the element of fire. You can almost see the flames of fire in its shape. Visualize the *shin,* take a deep breath, and, on the exhalation, make the sound of the *shin,* shhhhhh, extending it for the entire exhalation.

Now visualize the *mem* in the solar plexus, in blue light....The *mem* represents the element of water, bringing harmony to all levels of being....Visualize the *mem,* take a deep breath, and, on the exhalation, make the sound of the *mem,* mmmmmmmm, extending it for the entire exhalation.

Now visualize the *aleph* a few inches above the top of the head, in white light....The *aleph* represents the element of air. The *aleph* connects us to *Ain Sof,* God's light before creation. The *aleph* is silent.

Repeat the meditation on these letters at least three more times, each time allowing the letters to go deep inside.

Now, on the fourth time, when you say the *shin*, visualize that you are in the midst of holy fire. When you say the *mem*, visualize that you are immersed in the depths of water. When you see the *aleph*, visualize that you are floating in air. You may repeat this visualization a few times as well.

Now we will chant each word of the Shema as we did the letters. With each exhalation, chant each word of the Shema. When we say God's name for the first time, visualize the letters of the Divine name before you on your inner screen. Be aware that God is transcendent. He is other. He is outside of creation. When we say God's name the second time, place the letters of the Divine name inside of you. Visualize the *yud* in the head, the *hay* in the shoulders and arms, the *vav* in the torso, and the final *hay* in the waist and legs. Be aware that God is immanent. God is within creation. When we say the last word of the Shema, *echad*, be aware that God fills this universe: His presence pervades the six directions—north, south, east, west, up and down.

Chant the Shema with the *kavannot* (contemplations) prescribed above. With each exhalation, say another word. *Shema ... Ysrael ... Adonay ... Eloheynu ... Adonay ... Echod....* "Hear Israel, the Lord your God, the Lord is One. Listen.... God is transcendent, He is outside of creation.... God is immanent, He is within creation.... God is a unity. Everything flows out of His oneness.

"You shall love the Lord your God, with all your heart, all your soul, and all your might." ... Breathe into the heart.... Breathe into the chest area. Allow the heart to open to love, loving God and being loved by God.... As it says in the Prophets, "You are loved with an everlasting love." ...God loves you unconditionally. You are loved as you are. Open to receive this love. Breathe this love in and let it fill you....Sit in meditation drinking in the love and oneness of the Shema for as long as you want....If you like, repeat as a mantra an affirmation such as *Hashem echod* (one God), "I am loved and lovable," or "I am loved by God " ❖

9

On Being Loved and Loving

The Shema, in the traditional prayerbook, is sandwiched between prayers expressing God's love for Israel and the commandment for the Jewish people to love God. Only through love is oneness experienced. Love and oneness are connected. This is true in human relationships as well as with the Divine. The Hebrew word for love is *ahava*, and the Hebrew word for one is *echad*. In the kabbalistic practice called *gematria* the assignation of numerical value to letters makes a connection between words that share the same numerical value. Numerically, both *ahava* and *echad* add up to 13. There are also thirteen attributes of Divine compassion that Moses heard when he received forgiveness for the Jewish people's creation of the Golden Calf.

Our relationship with God is the most intimate, lasting, exciting, and loving relationship that we will have. It is also a mirror of our relationships with ourselves and with others, particularly our intimate ones. Love is a gift, yet it challenges us in very deep ways We are all challenged in our human relationships, as well as in our relationship with God. All relationships take work. They may bring many rewards, and our lives are enriched by them, but they also make many demands upon us.

What we believe about God often reveals what we believe about ourselves. If I believe that God is compassionate and loving, it is likely that I will be that way as well. The Baal Shem Tov used to say that God is our shadow. What we do, God does. If we move close to God, God moves close to us. If we move away from God, God moves away from us. If we are loving, God connects us to the root of love, and we become a channel for God's love.

When we open to greater love in our relationship with ourselves, with others, or with God, we expand our capacity to love. For example, the more loving we are to others, the better able we are to love God and receive His love. Similarly, the more we open to loving God in prayer and meditation the better able we are to love ourselves and others. We need always to remember and acknowledge that when we love and are loved by others, this love comes from God. We are blessed to have this experience of love, because all love is the love of God.

When I ask Jews to open to the experience of being loved by God, some feel that a loving God is a Christian concept, and that the Jewish God is not loving. Many Jews have told me this. I see this perception reflected in the patterns of religious observance and affiliation of my clients at a psychiatric clinic where I work as a psychotherapist. I have noted that most of the Christian clients, primarily Catholics, attend church regularly and experience consolation and support there. They believe that God loves and supports them. The Jewish clients, on the other hand—with the exception of a few religious Jews—are not connected Jewishly. They do not consider prayer or synagogue attendance as a source of support for them. This is tremendously unfortunate and a misconception.

There are many references to love in the Bible. Many sayings attributed to Jesus, such as "Love your neighbor as yourself," originally came from the Old Testament. However, when people read the Bible in English without commentary, they sometimes conclude that this Jewish God is angry, jealous, more punishing than loving. This is understandable, as there are many examples of God "punishing" the people. Consequently, many Jews wonder why they should want to connect with the Jewish God of the Bible.

Many people question the relevance of the Bible to their lives. If the Bible were just a collection of stories about people and events that occurred long ago, it would not have been cherished as a holy book throughout time. The Bible must contain something very profound to have captured the hearts and minds of so many people for so long. For most of us, on the simplest level, the Bible—or, the Torah, in Hebrew—becomes relevant and alive when we identify with the people and the teachings underlying the recorded events. Though our lives are different from those in ancient times, some things do not change. We can find ourselves in the stories. For example, we each can experience our own bondage, as the Jews experienced bondage in Egypt. We are also challenged to develop faith and trust in God, as the Jews who traveled through the desert were. We have our own golden calves to whom we bow down and dance around like the Jews in the desert. We can learn from the experiences of the people in the Torah if we identify with them. The Torah offers practical guidance for our life situation.

Judaism has produced many commentaries, as well as commentaries on the commentaries expounding on the Bible. The rabbis extracted laws and teachings from the written Torah. Torah is more than the five books of the Bible. In Judaism, there are five levels to deciphering the meaning of the Torah. We have to learn how to decode the Torah on each level.

At the deepest level, however, the Torah is considered a blueprint of creation. The secrets of life are contained within it. I like the image of the Torah as a woman who tests her suitors to see whether they truly love her. She will not reveal her depths until she is sure that they are trustworthy. She may even wear unattractive garments to repel insincere and unworthy suitors. A person must prove his sincerity before the Torah becomes intimate with him or her. The

Torah is also like a mirror of a person's soul, a person sees his own reflection there.

The Torah is divided into portions, and each week we read a specific portion. The weekly portion has a hidden message for you that is relevant to your life right now, but you need to know how to decode it. This requires effort, reflection, and prayer on your part. Sometimes I develop meditations around the Torah portions, but that is a subject for a future book. For now, if you want to explore the depths of the Torah, seek assistance from traditional commentaries and attend classes on the Torah portion given by a knowledgeable teacher. Some of the traditional commentaries on the weekly Torah portion have been translated into English. My personal advice in selecting a teacher to learn Torah with is to find someone who makes Torah learning exciting. If the teacher does not love the Torah and does not make the Torah sweet, it is better to stay home and study with a friend or by yourself. Learning the Torah is to learn about God. Learning about God awakens the love of God.

Without learning Torah and meditation, it is difficult to experience the love of God. The lack of loving role models, and the subjection to painful life experiences, may also challenge our belief and our love of God. Looking deeper into the hearts and souls of people, I have found that people's belief in God is not necessarily the result of painful life circumstances or religious knowledge, but depends on whether they feel lovable or worthy of being loved by God or anyone else. Sadly enough, many of us did not get the message from our parents that we were loved unconditionally. We have not yet experienced unconditional love in our intimate relationships. Consequently, many of us still live our lives according to limiting and negative messages about ourselves that we received very early in life.

Many years ago, I modified the popular "inner child" work to create a Jewish meditation to heal the inner child and bring this child to God-awareness. I use variations of this meditation quite frequently in my private practice. I have seen how this meditation transforms people's lives in direct and powerful ways. Prior to doing this meditation, you may want to find pictures of yourself as an infant and as a child and look at them. Share them with your meditation partners or group. This meditation is preceded by relaxation, centering, and self-observation.

Meditation on the Inner Child and Love

❖ Assume a comfortable seated position on the floor on a pillow or a chair. If you prefer, you may lie on your back. Allow your eyes to close. Let the belly be soft. As you inhale, let the abdomen expand, and as you exhale let the abdomen contract. Focus on breathing in this way.... This is a time to be with yourself in an intimate, loving way.

We'll begin with relaxation and a moment for self-observation.... Focus now on your physical body. Scan the body for any tensions, any holdings you may have.... Imagine that you can send the breath to any places of tension, and give the body permission to relax.... This is a safe time to let go of your physical armor.... Become aware of the face and let the muscles in the face relax.... Let the muscles in the neck and shoulders relax.... Now the arms and the hands relax.... Release all tension in the back and relax. Relax the abdomen, the buttocks, the legs. Let the entire body be relaxed. Take a few deep breaths and relax for a few moments.

Now focus on the emotional body without judgment. What are you feeling now?... Allow this moment to be time for awareness and self-acceptance.... Experience what you are feeling without having to explain, judge, or rationalize.... Just take note of what you are feeling. Be aware of any present concerns you may have. Ask yourself whether you can put them aside for this time of meditation.

Bring your focus now to the breath. Focus on the inhalation and exhalation. Begin to deepen the breath. Take long, deep breaths, inhaling and exhaling through the nostrils. Let each breath take you deeper inside....Allow yourself to relax....Go deeper inside. Follow the breath inward, and feel yourself going to the core of who you are....Travel to the most private, intimate place within yourself, a secret place inside where only you can go. In this quiet place inside, listen to the voice of your own soul....What do you want to express more fully in your life?...Sit for a few minutes with this question.

You will now be guided in a journey of the soul, a review of the descent of your soul to this physical world. You will have an opportunity to look at your life from a different perspective. You can review early decisions you made about God and yourself. Some of them no longer may be appropriate. God willing, this time of reflection will be a time of healing....a time to let go of limiting ideas of Who God is and who you are, and move to a deeper, more expanded, and truer experience. Take a few deep breaths, and during this meditation recall any memories, emotions, and impressions.

Imagine that you can go back to the time of your own beginning....It is said that at the time of your parents' engagement, or when your parents decided to come together, you looked down from the place of souls in the spiritual world and you chose these parents and the circumstances of your birth....Why were you attracted to those particular individuals who are your parents?

Visualize your parents as the people they were at the time of your conception....Who are they? ......Did they love each other?...What was their consciousness at the time of your conception? Were they ready for you? Did they wait a long time for you? Or did you come unexpectedly?. .Were they happy about your arrival?

Now see yourself in the secure physical place called the womb, where all your needs were met. Imagine yourself floating in warm water, safe and secure. Your soul gradually became accustomed to being joined together with a body. It is said that during the nine months of gestation the infant learns Torah. In the womb you were told what you were to do in this world. The memories are there, you just can't access them, but often you learn something, and know that you knew it before.

After nine months of being nurtured in this way, you were forced to leave and enter directly into the physical world....Your birth was a great miracle, and many people rejoiced. Your parents may have been conduits, instruments, for God, but God is your true parent. You now share in the mystery of life, just as your parents do. You are a child of God. Your parents are children of God, too....Yet you, as an infant, were now a little closer to God. See yourself as the infant you once were....You were so pure and innocent. You were absorbed and fascinated by the sensations of being in a physical body. How unusual, interesting, and exciting this experience was.

God made you so sweet, so alive, so helpless. Your parents could not help but love you as much as they possibly could. As an infant you were totally dependent. You had so many needs. You had such a need to be loved and to be held. If you had not been loved, you would have died. You also needed to be fed and to be changed....You needed a lot of attention.

When you expressed your needs and you cried, did your parents respond quickly, or did you wait a long time for your basic needs to be met?...Do you remember being wheeled around in the carriage, or in a back pack close to your parent's body? ...Did you have to share your parents' attention with siblings?...Were they close in age to you?...Did any of your siblings take care of you?...Did your parents play with you a lot?...Or do you remember being left for long periods of time in the playpen or crib?

We taught our parents a lot about what it is to love another person. Some of our parents really grew from this opportunity. Others were not quite ready to appreciate fully the gift they were given. Some were overwhelmed by the responsibility and the pressures. A few of them may have even violated God's trust. How did your parents welcome you into their lives?...Were you the center of their lives? ...Think of any unusual experiences of your infancy that you may have heard of or remember....Did you make any decisions about yourself or about life when you were an infant?

Now see the child you once were. In the softness of your heart, feel and see yourself as the vulnerable child ready to greet the world outside of the home. How old are you?...See yourself as a child eager to enjoy each moment, wanting to play, to laugh, to love, to enjoy life....See this playful child....Recall some experiences where you felt particularly playful or lovable as a child. Recall as much detail as possible. Visualize these experiences as if they were happening to you now....Experience the detail, the sounds, the smells. The world is so wonderful, so beautiful, so fascinating. Feel the sense of security, well-being, and delight of the child....This playful child lives within you today. Do you give him or her time to play? Affirm that you will give this child time to play in your life.

There were also times when you, as a child or infant, were hurt, when you were frightened, when you wanted to be held and no one was there. You may have been told directly or indirectly that it was not okay to be who you were. You needed to behave in a certain way to be loved. You may have been told to not feel the feelings that you felt. You may have even felt that your life was threatened. You may have been hit or beaten. You may have been told directly or sensed that you were not a good boy or girl or that you were not really wanted...You may have felt responsible for your parent's pain or for any conflict between your parents.

No matter how hard you tried to please your parents, it never seemed quite enough....Sometimes you felt so bad, that you cried, and you were told that you should not cry. Or you cried and cried and no one came. So you stopped crying. What happened to those tears?...Where did they go?...Imagine how hard it must have been for God to have entrusted you with your parents, who did not treat you like the prince or princess you were. Perhaps you felt God's presence with you. He was there with you....God inspired your parents to take care of you and to love you....He was constantly pouring out His love to you.

What happens to your tears today?...Are your needs met, or at least heard?...Take the time to listen to the child within. Ask your inner child to speak to you now....What do you need, little one?...Tell the child that you are there....You are ready to listen, to care, to love this child....Assure your inner child that you are now an adult and that you will take care of him. You will protect him. See your inner child before you. Imagine that you can hold this child in your arms and feel your unconditional love for this child....Tell the child that he doesn't have to pretend to be someone he is not before you....He doesn't have to keep his feelings from you....Tell your inner child that he is lovable, sweet, and beautiful. Say the following several times silently and then aloud: "You [your name] are lovable, and I am there for you." You will do the best you can to take care of this child. This child is your first priority to love, cherish, and protect.

Then repeat silently, "You are lovable, and God is there for you."...Tell this child that nothing he could do would make him unlovable. Tell this child that God is his true parent. With constant unconditional love, God is pouring out His love to him all the time. God has been taking care of him from the very beginning. God loves him with a perfect and unconditional love. If God were to speak of this love, what would He say to this inner child?

Know that, in the greatest moments of joy, God is with you. In the deepest moments of despair, God is there with you. You are loved....You are protected....God is your true parent. As a child you can call on God at any time. You do not need an appointment. No matter how far away you may feel, God hears every word you say. He is not limited to space. He is everywhere. No word to God was ever uttered in vain... Remember that your tears, your cries, are precious to God.... God will wipe away your tears....You are so beautiful. It is beautiful to be you....You are loved with an everlasting love....Be sure that your inner child really hears this assurance. Assure your child that you and God will protect her....Does your inner child really hear you?...Experience your inner child being reassured....Your child has a natural faith in God. Your child will also teach you about faith, love, and trust. Remember that God created this world for love. Your child knows how to love.

Imagine that you can see a movie of how love has unfolded in your life so far....Recall acts of love done for you and acts of love you performed for others....Recall people with whom you shared love. Let these images flash on your inner screen....Reflect on the gifts and growth opportunities these relationships provided. Do these people have anything in common?...Do you note any patterns?...Reflect on the joy and blessing of the love in these relationships....Reflect on how you may have been betrayed and hurt by love....Did you value the love that was given to you?...Were you generous and giving with loved ones?...Were you more concerned about what you received from others?...What have you learned about love and your capacity to love? Go to the present moment. Are you presently open to increasing and deepening love in your life? How does love manifest in your life today?...How large is your circle of love and caring?...How intimate?...How do you express your love to others?...How would you like to increase your capacity to love?...What have you learned about yourself and love?... When you finish, bring your attention to the breath, and when you are ready, open your eyes. ❖

Follow-up Exercise

After this meditation, take time to write in your journal any insights that you discovered during this meditation. It is a very healing experience to write your reflections on some of the questions posed. If you have shared this meditation with others, select a partner, and take turns sharing with each other. If you like, ask each other some of the questions listed above and take turns sharing.

10

Bringing Meditative Awareness into Daily Life

When beginning a meditation or spiritual practice, people usually focus on what they want to receive. They ask: "What are the benefits?" "Why should I invest my time and energy?" It is fine and appropriate to meditate, pray, and do a spiritual practice with the hope that you will be worthy to receive all the spiritual riches that you have heard the practice offers. I often begin a meditation session instructing students to come in contact with their intention for meditation. "What do you want to receive?" Desire and intention are important, and greatly affect the actual outcome of the experience. There are many benefits to meditation. Reflect on the benefits you have received so far in your practice of Jewish meditation, and on what you would like to receive from a continued practice.

At a certain point in our relationship with God, we have to ask ourselves whether we are takers or givers.? Do we want God only when things are good? Or do we want God only when things are bad? Do I really want to get close to God? If I am relating to God only as a "sugar daddy" who answers my needs and either gives me or doesn't give me what I want, I will always be separate from Him. He is the giver and I am the receiver. I may be happy with Him, I may be angry with Him, but there is a distance between us. As a person progresses on the spiritual path, what a person wants becomes more refined. The distance between him and God is painful. His deepest desire is to be close to God. This he wants more than anything else.

In the world of spirituality, closeness is measured by resemblance. The more things resemble each other, the closer they are to each other spiritually. A person becomes close to God by imitating God. As God is a giver, a man who is a giver resembles God and is close to God. One of the main ways we give to God or come close to Him is by surrendering our personal will and aligning ourselves to Divine will. In doing this, we can actually enjoy greater intimacy with God. This is a necessary step in spiritual growth.

In Hebrew, the word *bittul* is used to describe this state of self-nullification. It is only through becoming *bittul*, nullifying oneself, that we may experience God as God, not as a projection of our own fantasies. If we are full of ourselves, there is no room for God and what He wants to give us. If we are an empty vessel, we are open to receive. It is a spiritual paradox that the more we nullify ourselves to God, the more we actualize our true selves and the greater we become. Let's ask ourselves: "Am I willing to nullify my personal will for Divine will?" This is where Jewish spirituality and meditation starts to get exciting and maybe a little scary for some of us. "Am I willing to let go of limited ideas of who God can be and allow God to be God in my life?"

By becoming *bittul*, the barriers separating us from the divine are removed. The "I" of ego is replaced by the "I" of God. To make ourselves *bittul*, we need to meditate on what God wants for us and on how we can align our personal will with Divine will. We have to get out of the way, so to speak. We transcend our limited selves. We realize that our personal needs only limit our connection with the Divine. We want to connect with God not for the personal benefit, but in order to serve God for God's sake. Our desire is solely to be connected to God, not for what He can do for us. This is true devotion. We can understand this very clearly in the world of personal relationships. We love someone not because of what they give to us, but more because of what we give to them. Giving is the greatest joy. We want to be givers, not takers. As it says in the ancient and popular book, *Ethics of the Fathers*, "Do not be like servants who serve their master for the sake of receiving a reward." We are interested in doing for God, not in receiving from Him. Paradoxically, with this attitude, by self-nullification, we receive the most.

By becoming *bittul*, it is possible to access the infinite well of divine light and love. It is said that the more water the well gives, the sooner the well is replenished with new water. Similarly, the more love we share, the more love we have. In meditation, the more we give way to God and allow God to be with us and in us, the more Godliness and joy is revealed to us. This is our greatest happiness.

It is our egotism that separates us from God and our true selves and keeps us from receiving the highest goodness. At the same time, a person must have a strong, intact ego before he can transcend and relinquish it. There is a major difference between humility and low self-esteem. Moses was considered the humblest of men, yet he was the leader of the Jewish people. We do not usually associate humility with leadership and strength, but in Judaism they go together. If a person is truly humble, he experiences himself as an agent of God. On his own, he does nothing. He allows God to work through him. Therefore he can be confident and strong.

A person with low self-esteem will not be able to be *bittul*. He cannot let go of a self that he does not have. It is too frightening. Such a person first needs to build his self-esteem by doing good things. *Mitzvot*, obligations prescribed by Jewish law, are God's way of building a person's self-esteem while simultaneously breaking the ego and making a person *bittul*. *Mitzvah* literally means to connect. The more you connect to God, the more you will receive from Him. If you want to grow spiritually, take on a *mitzvah*. Make a commitment to a meditative discipline or spiritual practice. If you are not sure what to do yourself, explore what you may do with a spiritual friend, your meditation group, or a rabbi. If you are already committed to a practice, see whether you can comfortably increase it. Be honest about where you are spiritually. Don't compare yourself to others. Grow from where you are rather than where you think you should be. Don't take on more than you can integrate into yourself authentically. Yet, if you want to grow spiritually, know that you have to flex your spiritual muscles.

Be careful—if you take on too much, too fast, you can blow your circuits. Go slowly. Stretch yourself ever so gently. Periodically check to see whether it is your ego, not your soul, that is in the driver's seat in your spiritual and meditative practices. One must be careful, for it is possible for a person to take on the practice of *mitzvot* only to reinforce low self-esteem.

If the meditation experience has been nurturing for you so far, why not meditate on a regular basis? Just as we eat three times a day to nourish the physical body, Judaism recommends that we pray three times a day to nourish the spiritual body. The meditations given so far may be practiced on a daily basis. It is a good idea to do each of these meditations every day. You may wonder how you will have the time to do this, considering all the other demands on your time. It is not difficult to do these meditations in abbreviated form, if necessary. It also is not necessary that you do them in a formal sitting. I often do these meditations while doing my errands.

Each day you can easily do the following:

1. Practice breath awareness and self-observation. As you live your life, be aware of how God breathes into you a pure soul. Do this many times in the course of each day.

2. Reflect on how the events that occur each day are the "hand" of God. What am I learning about myself? How am I challenged to grow in this situation? How may this event, this challenge, deepen my connection and awareness of the Divine Presence?

3. Practice gratitude for all the opportunities to give and receive each day. Being grateful fills us with a sense of well-being and makes us more open to receive additional blessings.

4. Place yourself in the presence of God and yearn to be close to Him. Take a few deep breaths and absorb those vibrations of Divine love and light. God is where you are. Allow God to be with you. Place the letters of the Divine name before you wherever you are. Carve the letters out on your inner screen, then visualize that you breathe the *Yud* in to the head, exhale the *Hay* through the heart, breathe the *Vav* into the torso, exhale the *Hay* through the legs. Silently say the letters to yourself as you breathe them. For a few moments each day, be aware that God is before you and God is within you. See the letters on your inner screen and then within the body.

Before you do something, consider whether God would support this action. As you do your daily tasks and errands, take a moment to be aware of your breath and imagine that you are walking to do God's will. Imagine that you are walking to God.

5. Talk to God on an ongoing basis. Ask God for what you need. Ask God to bring you closer to Him and help you to be a better person. The more you talk to God, the better it gets. If you have an ongoing conversation with God, it will be easier for you to ask for what you need and want for yourself and others. You will consciously share more of yourself with God. For example, when you have a best friend, you share with each other every day, if possible. Every feeling, every thought, every action that is important to your friend, you want to know about. You want to share those things that are important to you with your friend, as well. Because you are in such contact with your friend, you can ask her for help. Better yet, she knows what you need, and, because she loves you, she wants to help

you. It is the same with God. God is your best friend, the friend who is always available to you. You don't have to have an appointment once or twice a year. You don't have to wait to be in trouble. You are not a stranger.

When you go about your business and something happens that you have questions about or difficulty with, don't wait—talk to God about it immediately. If you have an interaction with someone and wonder whether you could have handled the situation better, ask God for help to refine your character and become a better person. I do this all the time. I am in constant conversation with God. I once heard a charming story about Reb Shlomo. One day someone saw Reb Shlomo walking down the street, and called out his name. Reb Shlomo looked up. He most probably thought that he had heard a voice from heaven.

6. At least once or twice a day say the Shema, and transcend the physical world for a few moments to taste the sweetness and joy of Divine oneness.

7. Make a commitment for a special time (or times) for prayer and meditation each day. Incorporate various *mitzvot* into each day.

The traditional way that the majority of Jews have meditated since the destruction of the Holy Temple has been to weave meditation into the traditional, set prayers. *Davening*, praying from the prayerbook, is the traditional form of meditation. If you have the opportunity to be in the presence of people who have taken on the religious practice of *davening*, you will notice that they often appear to go into a meditative state. Their eyes are closed, for the words are known by heart; the body sways gently or rapidly; and the breath gets slower.

Davening incorporates much of what we have learned so far. I know that many of you are alienated from the prayerbook. It has so many words, and there may be things in the prayerbook that you do not understand or agree with. You may think that you have to pray in Hebrew, and you don't know Hebrew. Feel free to pray in English. It took me a long time to be able to access the prayerbook. Now, if I do not pray each day from the prayerbook, I feel worse than if I did not brush my teeth. It is a nurturing experience for me.

I encourage you to purchase a prayerbook. It does not matter which one. Though I have not reviewed all the versions of *siddurim* (prayerbooks), I imagine that they all contain the same basic elements. I do, however, recommend the ArtScroll or Lubavitch, (Tehillat Hashem) editions because they include the kabbalistic intentions that have been excluded from the Conservative and Reform editions. Both have been translated into English.

The prayerbook is divided into morning, afternoon, and evening prayers. These prayers correspond to the times of animal sacrifices in the Holy Temple thousands of years ago. When the Jewish people lost the Temple and no longer could do the animal sacrifices, these prayers were said in place of the sacrifices. It was an innovative concept developed by the rabbis that words of the mouth, known as "lip service" in those days, could replace a physical act. Many of the prayers are words taken directly from the Torah or from the psalms of King David. The particular prayers were chosen because they encourage you to be aware of and reflect upon varying aspects of Godliness as you live each day.

Each prayer service has certain common elements. All three services contain psalms and the silent *Amidah* prayer. The *Amidah* is known as a standing meditation prayer where a person places himself as fully as possible in the presence of God. The morning and evening prayer services contain the Shema. Each service is structured so as to guide you to a meditative experience. I recommend that before you pray you take a few moments to relax and center yourself. Do the breathing and self-observation exercise for a few minutes. Place yourself in the presence of God.

The psalms included in each service are read to awaken the heart to love and yearning. Psalms traditionally were sung. It is inspiring if you can sing a psalm or two to a melody you know or have made up.

It is not necessary that you read all the psalms; it is better to read less and pay attention to the words and the feeling and awareness they convey. If some verse touches you, take it as a mantra and coordinate the repetition of the verse with the breath.

After the heart is awakened with love and awe of the Divine, we are ready to say the Shema. We now move from the realm of the heart and devotion to the realm of the mind and contemplation. Read the prayers before the Shema, and then chant each word of the Shema as you learned to do in Chapter 8 devoted to this prayer. If you have a few moments, sit quietly to absorb the Shema, to contemplate what oneness really means, and then say the prayers following the Shema.

The most meditative aspect of the traditional service is the standing *Amidah* prayer. Come to a standing position. Take a few moments to become aware that you are standing before God. Remember that if you were standing in the presence of a mortal king, you would try to be concentrated in what you have prepared to say; You should be that much more focused when you are aware that you are in the presence of the King of Kings, the Creator of the world. As much as God is the King, the Creator, know that He is not remote. He loves you with an everlasting love. He is very close and available to you.

You begin *Amidah* by taking three steps back and three steps forward. Centering yourself with the breath, take these steps very slowly and consciously. I use the three steps backward to become more aware and accepting of where I am standing in my life. I use the three steps forward to experience myself moving into awareness of being in the presence of God.

To make your *Amidah* experience more meditative, read the first paragraph very slowly. Take a long, conscious breath with each word if you have the time, reflect and absorb each word. When you say the first word *baruch*, or blessed, take a breath and reflect on the word blessed. What does it mean? Know that when we bless God, we open to receive blessing from God. The next word of the *Amidah* is *atah,* or You. Now we are addressing God directly. When you say God's name, you may want to visualize the letters of the Divine name before you. When we mention all the wonderful attributes of God, take a moment to breathe, feel, and experience them for yourself.

Each *Amidah* prayer contains a prayer for healing. This is when we call forth the people we know who need such a blessing. I may actually have a list of names with me when I *daven* or else I recall them from memory. It is customary is to say the person's Jewish name, daughter or son of, and his or her mother's Jewish name. If you do not know the Jewish name, feel free to use the English name. I say the people's names and visualize them with my eyes closed. I reflect on their pain they are facing now, how they really need this blessing. I then ask God to shine His light and love on them. God is always radiating light and love, but sometimes we are not open to receiving it. I imagine that I bring these people to God, and that they open to receive God's light and love. I see them happy and healthy and surrounded by God's light and healing. I thank God for healing them. I then say the final blessing: "Blessed are You, Lord, Who heals the sick of His people Israel."

There is another part of the *Amidah* where I insert a talking-to-God meditation. Each *Amidah* has the following prayer that begins, *Shema kolaynu,* ("Hear our voice"). This is the time to insert your prayers for yourself and for others' well-being and success. It is the time to request that your personal will be aligned with Divine will. It is the time to talk to God directly in your own words. After you have completed your conversation, close with the words: "Blessed are You, Lord, who hears prayer."

Toward the end of the *Amidah* is *Modim anachnu lach,* which is an expression of gratitude. This is a time to reflect on and be grateful for your personal blessings. If you are not easily filled with gratitude, ask God to help you discover blessing in what is happening to you. The *Amidah* ends by sending the blessings of peace to the world. The service is concluded with the *Alaynu* prayer, which is a visualization of a day when the presence and oneness of God is known everywhere.

The words of the prayerbook were written by the highest sages and prophets of Israel. These words have been recited for thousands of years by millions of Jews all over the world. These prayers form the cornerstone of prayer for Jews today. Know that by using these words you attach yourself to the Jewish community, and as such you can receive riches from the reservoir of spirituality accumulated by the community. It is a great gift.

Sometimes, when you say these words, your mind will focus on a certain word, and you will understand its personal meaning for you. As you become more familiar with the words and their meaning, you can more easily enter into a meditative state. At these times, you are paying attention not so much to the actual words, as to the delight of being in the presence of God and knowing that you bring the gift of these prayers, which have been prepared for you and said by millions of Jews for thousands of years. There are times in prayer when you may become aware that you are not doing the praying, but that God is praying through you. These are the most exiquisite times.

11

The Practice of Blessing

The practice of blessing is integral to Judaism. Judaism has a blessing for everything. We bless God for the physical activities in which we engage, such as eating, drinking, and even going to the bathroom. In so doing, we transform them into holy acts, make ourselves holy, and bring Godliness into the physical world. We say blessings for learning Torah, for healing, for livelihood, for travel. We bless our physicality and our spirituality. There are even blessings for hearing good news and purchasing new clothes. The most interesting blessing I have seen is the one said upon seeing more than 600,000 Jews together: "Blessed are You, Hashem, our God, King of the universe, Knower of secrets." These blessings are all in the *siddur,* the prayerbook, so you can easily begin to practice the saying of blessings.

The practice of blessing opens us to receive and channel an influx of spiritual energy. When we say the formula for most blessings, *Baruch atah Hashem* or *Baruch atah Hashem Eloheynu melech haolom asher kidshanu b'mitzvotav vitzivanu* (Blessed are You, Hashem, our God, King of the Universe, Who has sanctified us with His commandments), we say this blessing because we are commanded to do so when we take a certain action. When we say a blessing, we acknowledge the existence and power of God, and we align ourselves with God by doing this action. There is a beautiful story of a righteous person who said a hundred blessings each day. In the story he asked for an apple so that he could meet his quota of blessings for the day. Some people say blessings in order to eat food; others eat so that they can say a blessing.

There is a difference between prayer and blessing. In prayer, we ask God to do something for us; in blessing, we are channeling Divine energy. As most blessings begin with the words, *"Blessed are You, God,"* a person may wonder whether God needs us to bless Him. Why do we bless God? When we bless God, we ourselves are blessed. It is a gift from God that He allows us to bless Him. In so doing, we are able to receive from God in the most powerful way. When we bless others, we receive even greater blessing. Blessing is a powerful spiritual practice that is as uplifting to the practitioner as it is to the recipient.

When Abraham was instructed to leave all that he knew behind him, he received the following blessing from God: "I will bless you and make your name great, and you shall be a blessing. I will bless those who bless you and him who curses you I will curse, and all the families of the earth shall bless themselves through you." As Jews, we inherit the blessings of the lineage of Abraham, Isaac, and Jacob. We inherit the power of blessing. I do not imply that blessing is exclusively Jewish. Non-Jews also have the power to bless, but they do not do so with the formula and discipline for blessing prescribed in the Torah.

Blessing Meditation

You may do this meditation as you bless a person standing before you, or you may do it as you think about a person. If you are doing it with a partner, the person receiving the blessing focuses on the breath and on opening to be a vessel to receive the blessing. If you like, ask for a particular blessing you would like to receive.

❖ The person who is doing the blessing also focuses on the breath. First, exhale through the mouth, releasing tension and stress with the breath.... Then continue to take deep breaths, inhaling and exhaling through the nostrils.... Raise your hands to heaven, feeling that your fingers are spiritual antennas.... When you are relaxed and focused, visualize that you are transported to heaven and are seated in the Garden of Eden, where the Divine Presence is fully manifest.... Imagine that you are a *tzaddik*, a completely holy person, seated there with all the righteous of Israel. Soak up the vibrations of this setting. Suspend any limiting ideas of who you think you are.

You have the power of blessing. To do this, it is necessary that you nullify yourself, get out of the way, and allow the Divine energy of God to be channeled through you.... You know how to do this. It is a great pleasure to give way to God's energy and allow it to be expressed through you. Continue to take deep breaths. Feel that you can breathe into the top of the head. Imagine that the light of the *Shechinah* is above your head, entering you and surrounding you. Feel the energy in your hands.... Open to being a channel for divine blessings.... Visualize on your inner screen the image of a person you would like to bless, or see the person standing before you now. Consider what this person wants and needs, and open to bless her in ways beyond what she would request. Utter a blessing in your mind and then speak the words.... You may want to begin with these words: "May you be blessed _____" "May God bless you _____" or "You are blessed with _____," and continue to allow the outpouring in your heart and soul to be expressed.

If the person you are blessing is not before you, visualize that she is happy to receive your blessing. Say amen for the blessing you have just given. If you have received an actual blessing, say amen, for amen seals the blessing. Accept the blessing and thank your partner. ❖

Repeat this meditation with other people, and then take turns and become a recipient of the blessing. Doing this can be a great joy.

Follow-up Exercises

Blessing is a practice that we can engage in throughout the year. We transform our lives when we bless people and bless all that happens to us. Make it a practice to bless people. During the High Holiday period this will be very easy to do, as it is a common practice. If you have the intention and desire to bless people, there will be many opportunities for you to do so. Before blessing, quickly place yourself in a meditation state by recalling the previous instructions. You do not have to raise your hands, but it is better to do so. The hands are powerful conduits of divine energy.

If circumstances do not permit you to give a full blessing, find other opportunities. It is easy to throw a quick blessing into a mundane and casual conversation. Whenever possible, bring a friend's attention to God and to Divine Providence. Extend a blessing to him. Sometimes, when a friend is complaining or hurting, it is better to give a blessing than to give advice. When you feel the need, you can ask others for a blessing, or bless yourself. Be sure to say *amen* to a blessing, for this seals a blessing. If you want to receive a blessing, give to others. In many cities, we have plenty of opportunities to give charity on the streets, as there are many people begging for money. More often than not, the beggars extend a blessing to you when you give, and say: "God bless you."

A Chassidic story conveys an important teaching about the power of blessing. A woman visits a rebbe and asks for the blessing of having a child. The rebbe blesses her, and she leaves very happy and grateful. One of the top students of the rebbe is in the room, and witnesses what had happened. He then feels inspired to ask the rebbe for a blessing to have a child. The rebbe blesses him as well. Little over nine months later, the woman returns to the rebbe, carrying a beautiful baby, and expresses her tremendous gratitude to God and to the rebbe for his blessing. The top student is in the room when this woman returns to the rebbe. Having not had a child during this time, he inquires why her blessing for a child was answered, and his was not. The rebbe responds, "After this woman received her blessing, she went out and bought a baby carriage. Did you?" Of course, the student had not. The faith we have in a blessing and our willingness to act on the blessing is crucial.

Follow-up Blessing Meditation

It is a Jewish practice to say special blessings before and after eating food. This practice helps us to eat consciously, experiencing more fully the gift and pleasure of eating. This is heightened if we eat in silence, consciously chewing our food. In so doing, we can unify the physical and spiritual aspects of our lives. We can transform a mundane physical act like eating into a spiritual act by having the intention that we do this act with the consciousness that we are making a unification between God and the Shechinah.

I understood this on a very deep level when I was guiding my students during a Friday night Shabbos meal. After saying and meditating on the preliminary songs and blessings like *Shalom Aleichem*, which is the formal greeting of the Sabbath angels, and *kiddush*, a blessing over wine that affirms that God created the world, we said the blessing over the bread and ate in silence until we had dessert. I strongly encourage that you try this for yourself. Make your Shabbos table a meditative experience If you must speak, say only words of Torah related to the Torah portion or words from the heart and soul I can almost promise you that you will understand

Shabbos in a deeper way and that you will feel closer to the people you shared the meal with than if you had spoken to them.

To prepare yourself for a Shabbos meditation experience, practice eating as a meditative practice. This meditation can be done with any food. For our purposes here, take a piece of fruit—for example, an apple.

❖ Take a few deep breaths to center yourself. Imagine that you can go back to the time when the tree that bore this piece of fruit was being planted. Someone, in some unknown place, at some unknown time, planted a seed in the ground. Over time, the seed received a lot of water, much light from the sun, and fresh air, and grew into a sapling. The tree went through many cycles. Soon it was able to bear fruit. The fruit was picked, or it fell to the ground. This apple was packaged along with many others to be transported by trucks and purchased by stores, where you finally bought it.

Now hold this apple in your hands, appreciating the long journey it has made. Before we eat the apple, we will say the blessing, appreciating that God was the force in making this apple available to you. *Baruch atah Adonay* (Blessed are You, Lord) *Eloheynu melech haolom* (our God, King of the world) *boray prie ha etz* (Who creates the fruit of the earth).

Take a moment to smell the apple, and eat it very slowly without talking. ❖

12

Final Instructions: Finding a Teacher

This book is my giving over to you. I have not written about Jewish meditation, but have imparted to you the experience of meditation. These meditations and teachings come from my own personal experience as a teacher. This book is only an introduction to Jewish meditation; there is so much more to learn. I hope to write a sequel in the near future. A book is an unusual medium to communicate the depth of meditation, as it is the silence between the words which is important in meditation. This book is written with my prayers and love. I hope that you experienced that in the meditations.

Reb Shlomo often talked about the difference between teaching and giving over. Some people teach on the level of information; others give a teaching-over, and that is different. Such learning is much, much deeper. Here is my favorite story, which illustrates the difference between these two kinds of learning. It is also a story about meditation.

Reb Mendel Vorker was a holy rebbe known as the Silent Rebbe, because he never spoke. He would sit with his followers for fourteen to eighteen hours without saying a single word. Whoever was with him in the room was in a deep meditation. There was not a sound or a single movement. There was absolute stillness. At the end of the sitting, the rebbe would say, *Hashem echod* (God is One). Then he would say, "Happy is one who knows that God is One."

One day Reb Bereshel, a very wealthy man who was a disciple of the Vorker Rebbe, invited the rabbi of the city in which he lived to meet the rebbe. The rabbi, who prided himself on his knowledge of kabbalah, wondered why he should go to this rebbe, who was known not to speak. Most likely he thought, "What can be gained from someone who doesn't speak? What can I learn from such a person? This rebbe probably doesn't know anything; otherwise, he would speak."

After several invitations, the rabbi finally consented to visit the Vorker Rebbe. When the rabbi arrived, he went to the Vorker Rebbe's synagogue. There he saw very simple people, the shoemakers and water-carriers of the town, learning the *Etz Hayim,* one of the deepest kabbalistic books. The rabbi listened to them with awe, amazed that these simple people knew more kabbalah than he did. He realized that compared to them, his knowledge was minuscule. He was humbled. He reflected, "I am the chief rabbi in the town. I thought that I was a great kabbalist, but I don't know what the Vorker Chassidim know."

He confided in Rabbi Bereshel, who brought him to Vorker. Reb Bereshel then confided in him, telling him, "I know even more kabbalah than these water-carriers, yet I also know that I do not know anything next to my holy rebbe." They remained for Shabbos, when there would be an opportunity to meet the rebbe. On Friday night, the rabbi went with Reb Bereshel and waited in a long line to meet the holy Vorker Rebbe. Every Friday night, thousands of people came for Shabbos. The rebbe would look at you, and if you were lucky, he would give you his hand. That was it. He never spoke.

Afterward, Reb Bereshel went to find the rabbi, who was sitting in a corner crying. Reb Bereshel asked him, "How was it when the rebbe held your hand?"

The rabbi replied, "I always thought that I believed in God, but it wasn't real. When the holy Vorker Rebbe held my hand, it was revealed to me; I felt it. I knew that there is one God. There really is one God."

There is a big difference between a person transmitting the experience that there is one God and a person talking about it. Kabbalistic meditation was historically transmitted by the teacher directly to the student. It was a private transmission. For those who have tasted the true giving-over kind of teaching where you experience directly what the teacher is saying, it is hard to be interested in any other kind of learning. When you have tasted the apple and know its sweetness, it's hard to listen to people who merely describe the apple. There are spiritual depths that can be received only directly from another person. It is like reading a book about love. It is interesting, it is helpful, it may even be a road map, but it is not the same as having the experience of love.

Unfortunately, I have found that many people teaching Judaism do not teach from their own experience, but rather repeat all the shoulds of Judaism and imply that they, as well as you, are on such a low spiritual level that you shouldn't expect to have a spiritual experience. They do not give of themselves; they are judgmental. Time is too precious to waste it learning with rabbis who are angry, who put you or others down, who talk divisive politics, or do not make the Torah sweet.

If these comments remind you of the rabbi of your congregation, speak to him privately and tell him of your spiritual yearning. Ask him to speak of these subjects from the pulpit. Ask other people in the congregation to talk to the rabbi as well. Most rabbis are also spiritually hungry, that is why they chose to become rabbis. We can't realistically expect the average rabbi to be on the level of the Vorker Rebbe, but we can expect a rabbi to bring forth the teachings of those in the Jewish lineage who reached this level. Ask your rabbi to share with you his personal spiritual quest and how he has grown in faith and knowledge. Rabbis generally are very happy to hear of the spiritual hunger of people in their congregation, and very much want to support them in strengthening their faith and knowledge of God. Also ask the synagogue board to bring in guest teachers.

As a general rule, I believe that if you do not feel holier, more whole, more peaceful in a teacher's presence, he is not your teacher. You may gain some information from him, but find a teacher who revives your soul. Find a teacher who is loving and who loves you. Seek a teacher whom you can love and respect. Pray to God that you should find such a teacher, a rebbe. What is a rebbe? A rebbe connects you to your own soul. A rebbe is like a mirror, but he reflects to you the purity of your own soul. My criterion for a spiritual teacher, for a rebbe, is that learning with him opens my heart so that I am more in touch with my own soul. I feel love for him, and intuitively I know that he loves me even though I may not even be privileged to have a personal relationship with him. I have loved rebbes from a distance because I feel the Divine Presence just by looking at them, listening to them speak, or seeing them dance. To me, a spiritual teacher, a rebbe, is like an angel. He is a messenger of God for me. I feel the Divine Presence in the presence of a rebbe.

Know that the deepest teachings about God are transmitted without a word. A glance, a smile, a hug from a *tzaddik*—a righteous holy person—can take you to the highest spiritual places. I have had many such experiences. One of them occurred at the funeral of Rabbi Eli Chayim Carlebach, Reb Shlomo's brother and a devout, holy Jew in his own right. I attended the funeral along with hundreds of people in Boro Park, Brooklyn. As Reb Eli Chayim was a disciple of the Bobover Rebbe, the Bobover Rebbe attended. No words were spoken at the funeral. A few psalms were quietly said. As the body was taken from the synagogue to the car, I followed close to Rebbetzin Hadassa, the wife of Eli Chayim. For one moment only, the Bobover Rebbe looked at me. In that one glance, he penetrated my soul; I was seen and loved for who I was. I saw who he was. He revealed to me that he was a very great rebbe. That one moment was a taste of eternity, of holiness. In that moment, in that one glance, the rebbe assured me that he would take care of the soul of Eli Chayim now, as he had in life.

When I returned to Judaism, I was very close to Rabbis Shlomo Carlebach and Yitzchok Kirzner. These two men remained my rebbes until their deaths. I do not think that I would have been able to bear the challenges of being Jewish without them. I learned continually with them for many years. I always looked for opportunities to assist them in their holy work. I symbolically and literally sat at their feet. I received many blessings from my association with them.

If you do find a person who can be a rebbe to you, spend as much time with him or her as you can. You learn from the rebbe not only by what he says, but by how he lives his life. If you can't find such a rebbe, find a spiritual friend or friends with whom you learn and support each other's spiritual growth. Meditate and study together. Encourage each other. Share your spiritual quest with others. Find people with whom you can be spiritually intimate. Your choice of friends is very important.

In the absence of living rebbes who impart the God experience directly to you, call on tzaddikim who are living on the spiritual planes of existence. They are very happy to assist us. Many people routinely call on the God of Rabbi Meir Baal Haness (Meir, Master of the Miracle) in times of trouble. Many of our greatest teachers had maggidim, heavenly teachers. I can't help but feel the blessing of tzaddikim when I am teaching meditative kabbalah. A tzaddik is considered greater and more alive when he is not in a physical body and restricted by the physical world. Rabbi Nachman once said: "Better to be with a dead rabbi who is alive than a live rabbi who is dead."

Visiting the graves of *tzaddikim* is a powerful and important spiritual practice. Don't miss an opportunity to avail yourself of this experience if you are in New York or Israel. The Lubavitcher Rebbe is buried in Queens, New York, and the Satmar Rebbe's grave is located in Monroe, New York. Both are awesome and very accessible. You do not have to be a follower to go to their gravesites. I have heard that even non-Jews go regularly to the grave of the Lubavitcher Rebbe because the spiritual vibrations are so powerful there.

Every time I go to the grave of the Lubavitcher Rebbe, my life changes in unexpected, wonderful ways. Though I did not have a personal relationship with the Lubavitcher Rebbe when he was in a physical body, I do now. Being at his grave, I have had a glimpse of who he really was and have felt his tremendous and powerful love for every Jew and every person. I have taken many students and friends there, and no one has been disappointed. When you are there, take a deep breath; open your heart to God; speak to God; speak to the Lubavitcher Rebbe, do a little meditation; say a few prayers; and soak up the holy vibrations. Some Lubavitchers have adopted the practice of using the Lubavitcher Rebbe's previous correspondence to receive answers to personal questions. I call it Jewish "I ching." One simply asks a question and then opens to a letter in one of the rebbe's many books. The first time I did this, I received a blessing to write spiritual books. The second time I received a blessing to be a Jewish teacher. My students have done this, and they also have received guidance and blessings that were personally relevant.

I have friends who travel to Umman in Russia each year to pray at the grave of Rabbi Nachman. The trip is physically difficult and expensive, but thousands of people do this every year because it is so spiritually rewarding. Rabbi Nachman promised that if people went to his grave, particularly on Rosh Hashanah, and said certain prayers, he would intercede for them in heaven. Rabbi Nachman prescribed ten psalms as a remedy for any sort of problem, whether you are at his grave or not. The psalms are as follows: Psalms 16, 32, 41, 59, 77, 90, 105, 137, and 150.

Israel has many graves. The most frequently visited ones are probably the Tomb of the Matriarchs and Patriarchs in Hebron, the Tomb of Rachel outside of Jerusalem, the Tomb of King David in Jerusalem, Rabbi Yitzchok Luria in Safed, Rabbi Shimon Bar Yochai in Meron, the Rambam in Tiberias, and the Belzer Rebbe in Jerusalem. My rebbes Shlomo Carlebach and Rabbi Kirzner are also buried in Jerusalem.

PART II

Meditations for Self-Healing

13

Coping With Loss

We all have to cope with loss in our lives. Death, divorce, failed or painful relationships, and unmet expectations of self and others may continue to cause pain for many years after the actual event. Many of us hope that, through meditation, we will enter a spiritual realm where there is no sorrow and no conflict, only the experience of love and oneness. Meditative practices often provide a glimpse of Divine reality, and we are free from the pain; however, we soon must return to earth and be with ourselves in the mundane aspects of life. Meditation, however, is more valuable than providing merely an escape from pain. Meditation provides the spiritual fortitude to better deal with our challenges and better accept our losses.

It is not uncommon for people to view meditation as a way to suppress their feelings. The goal in many Eastern meditation practices is to remain neutral and unemotional. Judaism, on the other hand, has always welcomed a full expression of emotion. I recently had a new student who came to meditation classes and shared that she hoped that meditation would erase the grief she felt over her father's recent passing. I think that she believed that it was wrong for her to have these feelings. She was comforted when I told her that was natural and appropriate for a person to feel this way after such a loss.

The tears we shed, the pain we feel after loss in our lives, is actually a testimony of what this person or experience meant to us. If you have experienced a loss in your life, please do not repress your tears. Know that it is actually a privilege to weep over the loss of a loved one like a parent or spouse. Sometimes people come to me privately and to the meditation classes when they are going through a divorce. To go through a divorce is sad, regardless of the circumstances preceding the collapse of the marriage. The Gemara, the book of oral law in Judaism, says that the *Shechinah*, the Divine Presence, weeps after a divorce. If the *Shechinah* weeps, shouldn't we?

What is wrong with crying? According to Dr. Christiane Northrup, who publishes a health bulletin for women, it is healthy to cry. Tears contain enkephalins, which can dampen emotional or physical pain and release ACTH, which has a calming effect, through its action on cortisol, on our adrenal glands. Crying is a sign not of weakness, but of sensitivity and depth. In my clinical practice, I see many people who are clinically depressed and anxious because they don't cry. Terrible things have happened to them, and they isolate themselves from their own feelings and then from others. Too many of us have been shamed out of our tears because we were told when growing up that crying is a sign of weakness or manipulation.

I have experienced two types of crying. There is the crying that comes from the mind, from thinking negative thoughts. These tears are draining, leaving me exhausted, feeling depressed and sorry for myself. Then there is the crying that is deeper, which comes from the heart and soul. These tears make me vulnerable and open. Such tears may be likened to a portable *mikva*. The *mikva* is a natural body of water used for purification. How does a person get to the holy tears? Meditate. The tears we shed in meditation either from joy or from sorrow cleanse and open us to the deepest levels of our being.

To cry in prayer and meditation is a great spiritual gift. Many of my students have shed tears in meditation. This is a sign that the meditation has entered deep into their hearts. Rabbi Nachman spoke often about the preciousness of a broken heart. A broken heart actually allows the Divine light to enter a person's being. If a person is too sure of himself, too proud, there is a wall around his heart that prevents God from entering.

I keep emphasizing this because we live in a culture where the depth of feelings is not valued. We all received messages when growing up—women as well as men—that it is not appropriate to cry in public or even privately to ourselves. How often have you held a person in your arms while he wept or were held by another as you cried? Have you ever physically embraced another person while both of you cried?

In my view, these intimate and bonding experiences do not happen often enough. I remember only one time in my life when I cried that a friend held me and then we cried together. It was so special, so precious. Unfortunately, people do not cry together. Some of us may be uncomfortable in the presence of someone who is crying. Or we may be uncomfortable crying and showing our vulnerability to others. We may feel that we have to be strong for another person. Because people are afraid of other people's sadness as well as their own, we often comfort others by telling them to feel better and not to feel the way they do. We have all heard these words. "You don't have to feel that way," or "You shouldn't feel that way." How healing it would be if we could just be with each other's sadness. Are you comfortable in the presence of a friend's tears? How do you comfort another?

There are several Chassidic stories about rebbes healing through crying. In one story, a person comes to the rebbe and pours out his heart to him, crying profusely. The rebbe responds, "I do not know how to help you, but I can cry with you." They cried together and the man was helped. I like to think that in my counseling practice when I cry with clients, which I sometimes do, I am following in the footsteps of the rebbes who cried when they heard people's problems. In this way, we can all be rebbes to each other. We simply need to listen to and validate each other's feelings.

Some of us find it easier to cry to others, but we are afraid to cry alone. We are afraid of being overwhelmed by our sadness. Many people go to therapy to have a person to whom they can cry. Just having a person to listen is a great relief. Remember, when you are alone, that you can always cry to God. God is a large enough container for your tears. Your tears are precious to God. When you cry to God, you will find that God will comfort you. The Talmud says that sincere tears are the gates that open heaven.

The expression and release of our feelings in itself brings healing. Too many people anesthetize or distract themselves with things like alcohol, drugs, and sex to become numb and not feel their sadness. Fortunately, there are no harmful side effects to prayer and meditation, as there are with alcohol and drugs. Meditation and prayer will eventually heal you. You will soon be healthier and more joyous, and will feel more freedom in your life.

If you have experienced a loss, give yourself time to be with your feelings without judgment. Do not expect life to go on as if nothing has happened. Allow yourself time to feel your feelings. Your feelings are your feelings; they are not good or bad. You may feel sadness. You may feel anger. You may feel betrayal. You may feel guilt. Most likely, you will experience a combination of these feelings. Allow the energy of your feelings to go through you and be released. Do not label yourself weak or bad because you have certain feelings. Assume responsibility for your feelings, rather than resorting to blame. When you speak of your feelings, make "I" statements as much as possible. Show compassion to yourself as you would to a hurt child. Be patient and allow the grieving process to unfold in its own time. It is my deep hope that the experience in Jewish meditation will help you to treasure your own feelings, as well as others', more than you do now.

Before you do the meditation, I would like to share with you one of my college prayer-poems. This is my prayer and blessing for you. Through your pain, through your loss, may you open to receive God's comfort and consolation.

You answered my tears with the gift of Your presence. The pain has been replaced by a yearning, which grows greater with time. The more I taste, the more full I am and the more empty at the same time.

Let me enter thru the hidden gates.

Healing Meditation for Loss

❖ Assume a comfortable seated position. Affirm that this is a time to be with yourself in the most intimate and loving way. Light a candle for this meditation. Close your eyes and bring your attention to the breath. Take several deep breaths. Inhale through the nostrils and exhale through the mouth, making a sound like an ocean wave. Feel free to make any other sound upon exhalation. Continue to take deep breaths for a minute or two....Now scan the physical body....Take note of any sensations in your body. Perhaps there is a tightness in the chest or belly. Take a few deep breaths and direct the breath to the place of sensation....Open to the feelings contained in the sensation. Give yourself permission to be vulnerable, to feel your feelings. You may notice a place where your willingness to feel meets your resistance. There is a voice inside that says, "I am willing to feel that," and another voice that says, "I am not willing to feel this. This is too painful, too overwhelming." .Explore this intersection with compassion. . .Allow

yourself to be in that space, and soften the muscles of the body.
Take a few deep breaths....Relax and be open to your feelings.

Reflect on what your loss is....Feel your loss and all the
feelings associated with it. If you want, visualize the person on
your inner screen. Talk to this person about your loss. You may
even note some feelings of guilt, hurt, betrayal, and anger
mixed in with the sadness. That is natural. The more deeply
you feel, the more you will be able to let go and move on with
your life. Talk to the person you are now missing; take time to
be quiet as well. After the meditation, you may want to write a
letter to this person.

Continue to take deep breaths and raise your hands to the
ceiling....Call on God to hear your cry, to see your
distress....Ask that God comfort you, heal you, strengthen
you at this time of loss....Cry to God to help you....Now
feel that your fingers are spiritual antennas. You reach into
heaven for support. Continue to take deep breaths. When your
hands get tired, very slowly bring the hands down and wrap
them around you. Give yourself a hug....You are
loved....God says to you, "I love you with an everlasting love."
God's love is everlasting, unconditional. God will never leave
you....Breathe deeply and allow yourself to receive this
love. ❖

Healing Light Meditation for Loss

❖ Sitting in a comfortable position for meditation, take deep
inhalations through the nostrils and exhale through the mouth.
Do this for a minute or two, and then inhale and exhale
through the nostrils....Follow the breath inside. Allow
yourself to go inside yourself, to relax ever more deeply with
each exhalation....While maintaining your focus on the
breath, follow the exhaling breath as it completes itself deep in

the abdomen.. . .Explore the space between the breaths, that space after the exhalation and before the next inhalation begins. It is an empty, peaceful space.

Imagine yourself entering your private sanctuary....This is a miniature Holy Temple where the Divine Presence resides. This is a place of safety, refuge, simplicity, and beauty.... What does it look like?...What does it feel like?...What is in your sanctuary?...Imagine that you have in your sanctuary all that brings you consolation and comfort. What do you bring in to comfort you?...Who is there with you?

Within your sanctuary is a candle, burning brightly. Its flames flicker upward, continually dancing. Keep your eyes closed, or gaze at the candle burning near you with your eyes open. This light shines a message of love, eternity, and holiness. In gazing at this candlelight, you have a glimpse of God's light. This candlelight is the light of your own soul. This light comforts you. It gives you hope.

Light has the power to transmute darkness, negativity, and sadness. Let your sadness and hurt merge into the light.... Continue to gaze at the light. The more sadness and negativity you give to the light, the brighter the flame....Gaze at the light with your eyes open.

Now close your eyes and imagine that you are the light.... Your body is a candle and your soul is the flame....Feel the strength and brightness of your own light. Your light burns brightly....It consumes negativity, transmutes darkness. Stay in this meditation as long as you like. ❖

14

Increasing Self-Esteem and Combating Addictions

In my practice as a psychotherapist, I often see people who are wonderfully loving, beautiful, even brilliant, but who are unusually critical, punishing, and judgmental toward themselves. They may be highly accomplished in their careers—physicians, Ph.D.'s, successful businesspeople—but in spite of their external success, their self-esteem remains low. Deep inside, from messages received in childhood, they do not feel that they are good enough, lovable, smart, pretty, or deserving of goodness. No amount of personal achievement and success will, in itself, heighten self-esteem. All too often, these people sabotage themselves. They limit the amount of goodness they can accept in their lives. They see the negative in the situation rather than the growth opportunity. Often, they are involved in such kinds of addiction as alcohol, food, sex, etc. In chapter 9, "On Being Loved and Loving," we did a meditation which guided us to contact and embrace the inner child and bring the child to God. This meditation is extremely therapeutic and should be repeated often by people suffering from low self-esteem. In this chapter, you are given another perspective to understanding this problem of low self-esteem, as well as additional tools to heal yourself.

The *Tanya*, the book of Lubavitch Chassidus, says that a person's life is basically a battleground between the *yetzer tov* (the good inclination) and the *yetzer hara* (the bad inclination). We are constantly confronted with the need to make choices in our life, and we have many conflicting drives and competing interests vying for control. The battle occurs in the realm of thought, speech, and action. I am taking the time to describe the *yetzer hara* so you will be able to identify its influence on you and combat it effectively.

Rabbi Shlomo Carlebach said it is the *yetzer hara* (the evil inclination) that tells you that you are "not good enough," that you are "not worthy." Basically, the *yetzer hara* sends those self-deprecating messages that limit your spiritual growth and discourage you from following a spiritual path: "You'll never make it," "Who do you think you are?" "You're stupid." The *yetzer hara* is external to you, yet it acts as if it is who you really are.

Other, more traditional, teachers from the *musar* movement in Judaism say that the *yetzer hara* is the ego or our physical and emotional desires. Here are some of the additional characteristics of the *yetzer hara* so you can identify them. The *yetzer hara* is impulsive. It does not want to wait. Rabbi Yitzchok Kirzner would say if you feel that you have to do something right away, it is likely the voice of the *yetzer hara*. The *yetzer hara* leads you to do things that are clearly self-destructive. It wants immediate gratification.

The *yetzer hara* is very clever and very subtle. It often veils and disguises itself in moral imperatives. The *yetzer hara* is concerned that you receive the honor you deserve. Do people notice you? Sometimes people do good deeds because of the *yetzer hara*. For example, people sometimes give to charity because of how they will appear in the eyes of others. Where I grew up, the exact amounts of money people gave to the Jewish Federation used to be published. People who are aware of the power of the *yetzer hara* often hide the good they do because they want to protect themselves from the influence of the *yetzer hara*, which will try to claim credit for the good deed. The *yetzer hara* will say, "God, he really did this so others will think that he is so generous or so holy."

Often, the *yetzer hara* tries to prevent you from doing good to another person and even to yourself. It wants only to take. The *yetzer hara* always wants you to get something in return; don't give unless you can get something back. The *yetzer hara* is calculating. It does not matter how successful you have been in life. It is never enough. You are never enough.

Be forewarned and be on your guard for the intruding discouraging thoughts of the *yetzer hara* in your meditation and in your spiritual journey. Learn to identify him. The *yetzer hara* is very seductive. The *yetzer hara* may tell you that he is watching out for you. He is protecting you while he leads you down a path of self-destruction. The *yetzer hara* is clearly the voice of addiction. One of my clients at the clinic described his father, who had a gambling addiction. "If my father was in the desert, thirsty, and there was either a glass of water or a lottery ticket, he would take the ticket." This is the *yetzer hara* at work.

The *yetzer hara* causes you needless worry and anxiety. If you are filled with worry and anxiety, know that the *yetzer hara* is at work. If you are involved in self-destructive activity and you have difficulty changing your behavior, this is the work of the *yetzer hara*. If you are very critical of yourself and judge yourself and others harshly, this is the work of the *yetzer hara*. Judging keeps you stuck in a negative pattern. It makes you feel powerless to really change and become a better person. Stop judging yourself as a bad or worthless person. Start to do good things for yourself and others.

In your meditations and in your life, take note of the various voices speaking in your mind. Can you identify the influence of the *yetzer hara?* You may thank him for sharing, and then dismiss him with a long, deep breath. Try not to give the thoughts of the *yetzer hara* a resting place in your mind. If these thoughts do not capture your mind's interest, they will fade away. *You have the strength to overrule the yetzer hara.* Do not engage in an extended battle with the *yetzer hara;* that only gives him energy and power. The *yetzer hara* may ask for a small concession from you. This is like giving one small drink to a recovering alcoholic. Remember, the *yetzer hara* deals in illusion, which he masquerades as truth. He has no real substance. Truth instantly dispels falsehood, just as light immediately pushes away darkness. All the meditations we have done weaken the *yetzer hara.*

When you feel that you are mired in a negative thinking or feeling pattern, deepen the breath, particularly the exhalation. Let go of your critical thoughts with the exhalation. Be reassured and take comfort that the limiting and negative ideas you have about yourself will be healed and transformed through the practice of meditation. God gave us these two inclinations, and instructed us in the Torah on how to channel the *yetzer hara* for our highest good. We can convert and channel the negativity of the *yetzer hara* in a positive direction and become stronger and better people than before. Remember that God is the most powerful energy, and you are a part of God. Know that through prayer and meditation you are rescued from the *yetzer hara* and actually gain control of your life.

In this meditation we will replace the *yetzer hara*—which, for our purposes we'll say is the voice of the "inner critic"—with the "inner caretaker," which is the Divine soul. Let me explain how this meditation works. In beginning meditation, people often enter a trance state. This is a state between normal waking consciousness and sleep-dream consciousness. It is the entrance to the domain of the soul. When you enter a trance state, it is actually a sign that you have opened to the subconscious mind, and the deep healing and inner transformation have begun. It is an optimal time to nourish the subconscious mind with positive visualizations and affirmations.

A trance state is like a hypnotic state. You may experience a gentle calm, inner tranquility, and great receptivity. You are open to receive on deep levels of being. Repeating an affirmation with the breath allows the affirmation to enter the subconscious mind and change implanted negative beliefs about the self. Remember that affirmations are true statements about the Divine soul that is your true identity. Repeating this meditation on a regular basis is a powerful way to transform the limiting or negative self-concepts. Do it as often as possible. If you want, you can even make a tape of yourself repeating your affirmation.

Affirmations are powerful. Many years ago, I repeated an affirmation with my breath for about five minutes each day for a month. My affirmation was, "I am lovable and loving." Within a very short period of time, several people unknowingly repeated to me the very words of my affirmation: "Mindy, you're so lovable and loving." I thanked them and smiled. Little did they know. It was a sign that my meditation work had been successful. I could stop and do something else. Most important, I now experienced myself in this way.

Affirmative Meditation

❖ Assume a comfortable seated position and focus your attention on the breath. Take a few deep breaths to release tension and stress....Take a few more breaths, inhaling and exhaling through the nostrils, allowing yourself to go deep inside, relaxing with each breath....Allow the mind to be quiet, and hear the words of the Bible said by God: "Let us make man in Our image and likeness."...You are created in the image and likeness. Rabbi Akiba reminded us that not only did God create us in His image and likeness, but He told us that He did this. This was a great gift....Repeat this to yourself several times with each breath. "I am created in the image and likeness of God." .If you want, say this aloud or even sing it aloud.

Compose a personal and simple affirmation about yourself or your life. If you can't think of something particular, feel free to use one of the standard, almost universally applicable ones, such as "I am loving and lovable," "I deserve love," "I am beautiful," "I am a child of God." If you prefer, repeat a verse from Psalms like a mantra, for example,"God is my light and salvation," or "Sing to God a new song." The psalms are filled with affirmations. Or say a simple "God is" statement, such as "God is with me." Coordinate the affirmation with the breath. These affirmations are true. They express the qualities of the soul or of the Divine....As you breathe in, repeat your affirmation....As you exhale, repeat the affirmation.

It is likely that, in the repetition of the affirmation, you may hear the challenge of the *yetzer hara*, asserting itself. Take a deep breath and bring the focus back to the positive affirmation....You may change the affirmation to the second person and say, "You [insert your name] are _____," and repeat the affirmation several times. Finally, say the affirmation in the third person: "She [Your name] is _____," and repeat the affirmation. Repeat this affirmation with the breath for a minimum of ten minutes. Repeat this meditation frequently. ❖

Follow-up Exercises

If you do this meditation with other people, the group should take turns saying aloud each member's affirmation in the second and third person. Each person should express his affirmation in the first person to the group. This is a powerful experience. Do not deprive yourself of it.

It is also a good idea to do this meditation as a writing exercise. Divide a blank sheet of paper with a line down the middle. On one side of the paper, write your positive affirmation. Now listen to the voice from the other side and write down what it says. For example, an affirmation may be, "I am lovable." The negative voice may say, "No, you are not." Continue this exercise until you truly believe that the positive affirmation is an expression of your essence and potential, and that the negative voice is a product of your fears and is peripheral to who you are.

Another way to increase your self-esteem and combat addiction is to perform acts of kindness for others. Become a giving person. Make offerings in small ways at first to develop your capacity to give. Give to people in need. Give for no reason. Giving is a spiritual discipline. It takes practice and commitment, just like any other discipline. It is by the act of giving and sharing that a person refines his character traits, overcomes selfishness, and transcends his fears and limitations.

When we do good things for ourselves and for others, we experience a greater sense of well-being. We feel good about ourselves. When we feel good, it becomes easier to make good choices. When we connect to the source of goodness, to God, we are empowered and enabled to do more good. If you start to feel resentment in giving, you are giving too much. When you give to others, you open the channels for you to receive from God. As God is a giver, you become closer to God. By giving to others, you become Godlike.

The kabbalah says that there are two basic drives in a person. One is the drive to take for oneself, which is the *yetzer hara*, and the other is the drive to give and share with others, which is the *yetzer tov*. Taking for oneself generally keeps a person isolated and bound to the demands of the ego and the physical body. The drive to take comes from lack of trust and the fear that there is not enough. A person who is basically a taker never feels that there is enough. He may give to others, but he does so only because he hopes and expects to receive from them. His true motivation in giving is not to give, but to take. A taker can't receive from others, because he suspects their motivations in giving. He believes that they give only to receive, as he does. He can't receive from God, either. He may even be religious, but he does his religious observance out of fear of punishment, or for the material and social benefits he obtains from religious observance.

On the other hand, a person who is basically a giver or who wants to be a giver experiences the joy of giving in and of itself. He can also receive from others. He recognizes that even in receiving he is giving, because in receiving he allows another to give. One of my friends informed me that she keeps a diary of the acts of kindness she does each day. In so doing, she is mindful to make an effort to do good deeds each day. She can read it over and feel good about the things she did to help other people. What a great idea! Don't forget to do good things for yourself as well.

15

Coping With Unemployment

We live primarily in a world of action, where we feel that we make things happen. Because God is concealed in this world, it is easy to believe that we create our own reality. We hear this slogan so often in today's spiritual marketplace. For example, we generally think that the amount of money we have is related to the effort we generate in order to make money. We are told this repeatedly, but Judaism says that the amount of money you have is from God. It is determined on Rosh Hashanah. A person can work very hard to amass a lot of money, and then lose it inexplicably. A person can make little effort and be very successful. For some people, money is a blessing; for others, money is a curse. We cannot judge our worth according to the money we or others have.

Unemployment can be a time of anxiety and crisis for many people. It is startling that people are often consumed with visions of becoming homeless and abandoned by even the possibility that they may join the unemployed. Needless to say, self-esteem is severely challenged during unemployment. We gain a sense of identity by the work we do. Without work, who are we? Many times people come to meditation classes or therapy because of the anxiety related to their unemployment.

For example, a rabbi came to me recently, expressing her anxiety about not having a rabbinical position for the next year. I comforted her by telling her that everything would be all right. Now she had been given a spiritual opportunity to deepen her faith and trust in God. Since she had been a former meditation student with me, I suggested that she view this time in her life as similar to exploring and meditating on the space between the breaths. Just as in meditation, she should explore and open to this empty space in her life. Even though she was still working as a rabbi, she feared the possibility of becoming inactive. She most likely hid a lot of anxiety in her busy-ness. She would have to face the fear and emptiness she felt inside.

I further advised her not to rush to accept any job, but to find a position that would allow her the opportunity to express her essence. She might be tempted to take a wrong position because she believed that she needed the money. If she did that, she would most likely find herself in a similar situation, learning that she needs to be true to her inner self. Incidentally, in a short time, she found a rabbinical position more suited to her needs and talents than the one she left.

I tell my students who are unhappy or, worse than that, feel exploited and abused in their jobs that they should consider leaving their positions. If a person has done everything he can to rectify the situation and still has been unsuccessful, he does not need to subject himself to abuse. This is not what God wants. We need to trust God and ask Him to provide and guide us to the right situation. We all need to work, but remember that we do not work just to earn money; we all need to work because we need to learn things about ourselves and others. We need to contribute, to give, to be part of something larger than ourselves. Work allows us to grow and express ourselves and bond with others in ways we would not otherwise.

We have to realize that it is not through our physical effort that we affect our lives the most. Judaism says that the spiritual arena is where we can make the greatest difference in our own life and in the lives of others. Our relationship to the Divine will ultimately makes the difference in the physical and spiritual realms of our lives. The proverb says, "Everything is in the hands of Heaven except the fear of Heaven." We need to trust that meditation and prayer are the keys to our success. We need to open to the goodness that God wants to give us. People who pray and meditate may do less and accomplish more. I often remind my students and myself that the brief time we devote to prayer and meditation will do more for us spiritually and materially than if we had not used the time for prayer.

I tell myself, my students, and my clients that when we believe in God we believe in Divine Providence. We do not have to be resigned to the laws of the marketplace. For example, a sixty-year-old woman came to my psychiatric clinic. She was very depressed because she had been told that she was going to be laid off from the bank where she had worked for the last twenty years. She couldn't keep herself from crying. She was so disabled by the news that she was unable to return to work. She was a devout Catholic who attended mass twice a day and did volunteer work for her church. With just a few sessions of counseling, she began to live her faith and trust in God and see the hidden blessing in her dismissal. She is presently considering being a foster mother or working in a day-care center, where she would do something more personally meaningful than her current employment in the bank.

Meditation for Unemployment

❖ Assume a comfortable position seated on a chair or cushion. Take a few deep breaths....With each exhalation allow yourself to relax deeply....This is a time you have given yourself to be with yourself in a nurturing, loving way. Continue to take deep breaths through the nostrils, inhaling and exhaling through the nostrils. Explore the empty space between the breaths. This space is empty, yet is quiet and full.

Reflect on how this period in your life is empty and quiet like the space between your breaths. This is a time of spiritual opportunity for you. You can attune yourself to God more deeply and explore yourself and get to know yourself in a new way.... Know that you are being taken care of.... God is taking care of you right now.... Breathe in this support.... Repeat with the breath this verse of the psalm, "My help comes from God who is the creator of heaven and earth.

"If you are unclear about the kind of work you should be doing, ask God what your work should be. Consider the activities you like to do. Ask that you be given work that will enable you to do what you like. Take deep breaths and listen to any ideas that come forth in response to your questions. ❖

16

Coping With Physical Pain and Serious Illness

A student recently described the intense abdominal pain she experienced during meditation. Because she was in class, she continued to meditate even though it was difficult for her to do so. She reported that the pain, which had been very great, soon became "sweet," and then it vanished. It is quite common for people who have or develop headaches and other bodily discomforts when they begin meditation to find that these pains have left them before the meditation is over. If you are in physical pain, do not fight it by tensing and contracting your muscles; doing so only increases the pain. Take long, deep breaths and relax. Be with the sensations. Breathe gently into the sensations. Ask God to take the pain away. Affirm that God is with you. Read psalms, particularly nos. 6, 31, 77, and 102. Do the "Let there be light" meditation often.

Reflect on what this pain or illness has to tell you. Why do you think you have a particular pain or discomfort? Do not judge yourself, making yourself feel guilty because you are ill or in pain.

Consider that there may be something to learn about yourself from this pain or illness. What have you learned so far in your recovery? Your pain or your illness is not an accident. Sometimes it is as a direct result of our actions that we suffer physically. For example, if we are diabetic and we do not watch our diet, we can easily make a connection between our illness and our actions. It is clear, and we can see it. Other times, it is not so clear or knowable. If you are in pain, it is more important to focus on how you can heal yourself and how you can grow from this experience than to spend time and energy blaming yourself for being sick.

What can you do to heal yourself now? It is your responsibility to explore, learn, and experiment with many healing modalities until you find what works for you. Be assertive. It is our natural birthright to be healthy. If you are not feeling well, seek help. Don't settle for living with pain unless you have done everything possible to help yourself. If a physician tells you that nothing is wrong and you still do not feel well, keep looking for someone who will help you. If one physician fails to help you, find a physician or an alternative healer who will help you. Keep looking. Be open to all your options. Ask your friends if they have any resources that may be helpful. Your help may come in ways that you may not have expected. Be proactive in your health care. Be sure that you are eating the most nutritious, life-sustaining food. Drink good water, and take the time outside to breathe fresh air and soak up some sunlight. Try to exercise and meditate as much as possible. Remember that God wants you to be healthy. Pray that God brings you the right people who can help you. I always say a prayer before seeing a physician that he should be God's agent to heal me. Finally, visualize yourself happy, healthy, and radiant. Always maintain hope.

Believe in the possibility of miracles. While we must respect the laws of nature and work with the laws of nature in healing, remember that God is the underlying force in your healing. The laws of nature can be changed if it is Divine will for that to happen. It does not matter how bad your prognosis is. If you are really ill or in considerable pain, ask people to pray for you. Give charity and do something to help others.

Healing Meditation

If you have a tape of soft, soothing music to listen to for meditation, turn it on. Light an aromatherapy candle.

❖ Lie on your bed or on the floor. Begin by feeling the support of the bed or the floor. Allow your body to relax. Take a few deep breaths in this position, inhaling and exhaling deeply. Make any sound you like to release your pain. Feel free to groan or sigh with the exhalation. Let it out.

We'll begin with a progressive relaxation of the body. When I mention a body part, bring your awareness to that part of the body. Explore any sensations present there. Listen to any messages this part of the body may be communicating, and then tighten the muscles around this body part and release with a deep exhalation. Your body is talking to you through sensations. Take a moment to appreciate each part of the body.

Now bring your focus to the right leg, explore the sensations there, and then tighten those muscles.... With a deep exhalation, relax the right leg.... Repeat this process with the left leg. Tighten the muscles and then relax the left leg.... Take a few deep breaths. Now bring your awareness to the buttocks and pelvic genital area.... Explore this part of the body. Tighten those muscles, and with an exhalation release those muscles.... Now bring your attention to the abdomen. Breathe into this center.... Explore any sensations there.... Tighten the abdominal muscles. Hold and exhale with a deep exhalation.

Now bring your awareness to the shoulders. Tighten the

muscles there.... Bring the shoulders up, bring them forward, and then release them with a deep exhalation.... Take a few deep exhalations and relax. Bring your awareness to your face.... Tighten the muscles there, and then release with an exhalation.

Repeat "My body is relaxed".... Continue to take deep exhalations to release any remaining tensions. You are relaxing your body because this is the best way for your body to be healed.... Ask God to heal your body.... Repeat with the breath several times, "God, please heal me," or "May the light of the Shechinah heal me now." Better yet say, "I now open to receive God's healing light and love," or "I am now being healed by God's love and light."

Imagine that your body is surrounded by God's healing light. Take deep breaths very slowly.... Feel free to make any sounds with the exhalation.... Relax the body as much as possible, for doing so allows the natural healing energy of the body to move freely in the body.... Imagine that breath goes particularly to the area of the body where you experience pain. Take slow, deep inhalations and equally deep exhalations. Visualize that this part of the body is healing.... See yourself becoming stronger and healthier right now.... Recall how you were once healthy, and visualize yourself as healthy now.... Affirm that you will never take your health for granted.... See yourself as healthy and free from pain.... Promise God that you will make a greater contribution to helping others when you are well and healthy. ❖

An Alternate Healing Meditation

❖ Assume a comfortable seated position or a position on your back. Take a few deep breaths to relax and center yourself.... Now come into the awareness that you are in the presence of God. There is no place where God is not. God is where you are right now. We are taught that the Shechinah, God's presence, is particularly close to someone who is ill....The Shema, as we learned, is an affirmative statement reflecting the highest truth, the highest consciousness. *Shema Israel Adonoy Eloyhenu Adonoy Echod*—"Hear O Israel, the Lord your God, the Lord is One.

Say out loud, taking deep breaths between each statement, and then repeat silently to yourself: "God is the one true and real force in this world....God is the one true and real force in my life....God is the source of all healing...God is whole....God is one....

Take a few deep breaths and affirm that you, as a human being, reflect God's divinity. Say to yourself silently several times as a mantra, slowly taking periodic deep breaths, and then say aloud: "I am created in the image and likeness of God....I am a part of God....As such, I am whole....I am healthy....My body and soul are in perfect alignment and harmony....I now see myself healthy, happy, and living life fully. This is God's vision and my vision....This is the truth....I breathe this truth into me. I accept this truth into the core of my being. I release any fear, doubt, or negativity that separates me from this truth....I thank You, God, for this healing. Blessed are You, God, who heals the sick. Amen." Sit in meditation for as long as you like. ❖

17

Insomnia

Insomnia, the inability to fall asleep quickly or to stay asleep, is a common phenomenon. The problem often occurs when people are very ill, in physical pain, or under intense emotional stress. Most of us have experienced it at some time in our lives. Sadly, there are people who struggle with this problem on a regular basis and frequently resort to sleeping pills, which does not always prove effective.

Sleep is very important. Our bodies, our minds, and our souls need the benefit and nourishment of a good night's sleep. Though we sleep part of each day, it is still a mystery how we sleep and what happens to us during sleep. Each day we have to surrender to a force that is beyond us. Each day we have to let go. Fear is often one of the reasons that we can't sleep. Trust and faith in God will help us to relax. All the meditations we have done thus far should, incidentally, help you to sleep better.

Praying, meditating, reading spiritual books, and reciting psalms will help you to sleep. If you need to, find some homeopathic remedies for sleep, or herbal remedies like valerian root. Visit a good health food store and ask the manager to recommend a natural sleeping aid. Drink soothing herbal teas. I have also found it helpful to turn off my telephone at least one hour before I want to go to sleep. Talking on the phone stimulates me, and then I have difficulty sleeping. The sages developed a short prayer and meditation service to cradle the soul away from the body and help the soul ascend to the spiritual worlds as it wants to do so much and does during sleep. You may want to read this bedtime service in the ArtScroll *siddur* before sleep, or to do the following variation of it.

Meditation for Sleeping

❖ Find a comfortable position lying on your back in your bed. Focus your attention on your breathing. Take deep rhythmic breaths, inhaling through the nose and exhaling through the mouth. Allow the body to relax. Feel the support of the bed. Give yourself permission to relax more deeply with each exhalation.

Now become aware of your physical body. Give yourself permission to relax the body. As the body relaxes, it gets heavier and heavier. The body melts into the bed. Repeat "My body is relaxed." Scan the physical body. Where you note any remaining tension in the body, take a few deep breaths and give permission for that part of the body to relax.

Now become aware of your emotional body and what you are feeling. Take a few deep breaths and let go. Repeat "I put my problems in the hands of God" and "Behold the Guardian of Israel neither slumbers nor sleeps" three times....Repeat "May God bless me and safeguard me" three times. Repeat "God, I long for your salvation". three times. Now repeat "In the name of YHVH, the God of Israel, may the angel Michael be at my right, Gabriel at my left, Uriel before me, and Raphael behind me, and above my head the Shechinah" three times.

Say once *Shema Yisrael Adonay, Eloybeynu, Adonay Echod* (Hear O Israel, the Lord our God, the Lord is One"). And sweet dreams. If you make the effort to record your dream, your dreams will become more vivid and meaningful. You give a message to the subconscious that what it says is important to you. ❖

18

Confronting Adverse and Challenging Situations

Frequently, in my private practice, people are confronted with particularly challenging situations. They feel the need for additional spiritual protection and strength. They have to go to court, face an ex-husband, or deal with some very stressful situation. King David, in the book of Psalms, says that "God is a shield to all who seek refuge in Him." Psalms is filled with prayers and meditations to help a person face difficult situations. During times of unusual stress, the following psalms are recommended: nos. 90, 3, 5, 9, and 25. Remember that inviting God into your life, particularly into the challenge you are now facing, is the best way to receive His protection.

Strengthening-Shield Meditation

❖ Take a few deep breaths to center yourself. Ask God to be with you and protect you in this time of distress or trial. Repeat

the verse of psalm 90: "God is my refuge and my stronghold."
Imagine that you are behind the shield of Abraham. "God is my
shield and my protection, whom shall I fear?"

If you are in need of strength, see the letters of God's name
Elohim, which is the name of God associated with the divine
emanation of strength known as *gevurah*. Say this name of God
silently to yourself. Wear the color red or visualize yourself as
surrounded by the color of red. This quality is associated with
the left arm and hand....Breathe in the energy of *gevurah*.

If it is your practice to put on *tefillin*, imagine yourself
wearing *tefillin* wrapped around the left arm and the
head....Now bring the thumb and the second finger of the left
hand together. This second finger is also associated with
gevurah. ...Anchor this meditation by holding your fingers in
this gesture. You will then be able to call forth this meditation
when you are directly confronted with your challenging
situation.

If you are in need of endurance, visualize before you the
Divine name of *Adonay Tzevaot* associated with the divine
emanation of victory. Wear the color light pink or visualize
yourself surrounded by light pink, as this is the color associated
with this divine emanation....Bring the right thumb together
with the right pinkie....According to kabbalah, the energy of
endurance is embodied in the right pinkie. Anchor this
meditation with this posture. ❖

Facing Challenging Situations

❖ After centering yourself with the breath, become aware of a
challenging situation you are facing in your life right now.
Reflect on the teaching and spiritual opportunity of this
situation. "Now is a time in my life when I _____."

Complete this sentence in writing, thought, or speech. What qualities of the soul are you asked to demonstrate now in your life?

Imagine that you can breathe in the spiritual quality for which you have the greatest need in your life right now. It may be love, faith, strength, patience, compassion, hope, or some other quality. Breathe this quality inside of you with each inhalation. With the exhalation, allow this quality to sink deeply inside you. Fill yourself with this quality. To deepen this experience, surround yourself with a color associated with this quality. For example, the color white is associated with peace or love. ❖

Shorter Abbreviated Meditation for Protection

It is a good habit to do this meditation before any important venture or crossroads in your life. You can perform this meditation many times in the course of a day.

❖ Take a moment to center yourself. Pray that what you intend to do is God's will, and ask God to help you and be there in the act you are about to do. In general, the best protection we can have in life is to align ourselves with Divine will, asking always that the choices we make be what God would choose for us. Imagine that God is like a warrior who precedes you on your path, clearing away all obstacles. ❖

19

The Practice of Gratitude for Greater Joy

The practice of appreciation for the gifts of our lives promotes happiness, and a sense of well-being, and protects us from violating and losing them. Marriages often fail because of the lack of appreciation of one for the other. When we take something or someone for granted, we are in danger of losing it. Our ability to be grateful and to appreciate what we are and what we have in our lives allows us to attract and receive additional blessings while filling us with a deep sense of well-being. This meditation and the prescribed exercises will help a person to overcome depression and loneliness.

Gratitude Meditation

❖ Each day you are given opportunities to give and receive. Take a few minutes to review the opportunities that were available to you yesterday or today from when you first woke up in the morning.... Take note of all the giving and receiving you experienced that you might otherwise have taken for granted had you not reflected upon it....It may be deep and profound, or it may be very small—for example, a storekeeper smiled at you when he gave you your change....Take time to savor each interaction you had with others, with nature, and even with yourself....Did you open to give and receive the flow of Divine energy in each interaction?...After a few minutes of reflection, bring your attention back to your breath. Take a few deep breaths, and feel a sense of gratitude for all that you have given and all that you have received. ❖

Follow-up Exercises

1. Write down the highlights of this meditation in your journal and share them with others.

2. What do you appreciate having in your life right now? List at least fifteen things in your journal. After you have completed your list, take time to savor each item Read your list often, and particularly when you feel depressed or lonely.

3. What people do you appreciate having in your life? Have you told or shown them your appreciation recently?

Afterword

I consider it a privilege to have been given this opportunity to share with you in this way. I hope that I will be blessed to share meditation directly with many of you in the future. I love to travel to different communities to share meditation. Feel free to contact me directly at (212) 799-1335. I thank you for reading this book and for practicing Jewish meditation.

Through the practice of Jewish meditation, I know that you have become a better person. I know that you have tasted greater inner peace and joy. I know that you have been healed in many ways. And I know that you have greater love for yourself, for God, and for others. Many of you have a deeper relationship with God, and have taken on or increased your Jewish spiritual practice. I thank you for this.

Each of us, in our own way, has brought more Godliness into this world through the practice of Jewish meditation. Though you may have done the meditations in this book alone or with a small group, you were not alone in the spiritual realm. Take a moment to feel your connection to all the people who have performed the meditations described in this book. Feel the invisible threads of support that exist between us. Now feel your connection to the community of Israel, to this holy community that has been serving God and the world for thousands of years.

Judaism has a long lineage of *tzaddikim*, prophets, sages, and rebbes who are supporting us in spirit and whose teachings are available to us whenever we are ready. So much holiness. So much support. Open to receive. We have been given the Torah with clear instructions on how to be in this world. We have so many other holy books to guide and inspire us. We have the Shabbos and so many holidays, additional time to meditate and feel God's presence. We have so many holy people living today who are happy to teach us Torah. We can travel to Israel. What a great blessing that in our time we can easily go to the Holy Land and pray at all the ancient holy places! Just breathing the air of Israel is spiritually uplifting. There is great abundance now.

Feel love and extend a blessing to every person who is dedicated to bringing God's light into this world. We are spiritually linked to each other. You are an essential link in this chain. There are so many beautiful people Jews, and non-Jews, working on so many different levels to heal this world. Some of us work in a public forum and have the privilege to inspire many people; some of us are very private and very hidden. Who knows whose prayers and meditations open the gates of heaven? We are connected. We elevate and support each other wherever we are.

Know that when we pray and meditate for the sake of heaven, heaven supports us. We have been given the responsibility to fix and heal ourselves and the world. Of course, we do this not alone, but as individuals and as a community. We each do our part. Being together is what makes it possible to go through the travails in our personal life and in our communal lives. We are here to help each other realize our spiritual potential and become who we are. We are here to bring Godliness fully into this world. We cannot do it alone, no matter how self-sufficient we may like to think we are.

Jews need to mirror community and unity for the whole world. We are a very diverse community, yet we need to recognize that we are part of a larger collective soul. We cannot be at odds with each other and not hurt ourselves. All this bickering between the various branches in Judaism is painful. It is said that the Holy Temple was destroyed because we did not love each other, we hated each other for no reason. The antidote for senseless hatred is senseless love. Love for no reason. Create space within you to love everyone. Meditation will help you do that. You may not agree with what people do, but that is no reason to withhold your love from them. Let's judge less, and love and respect each other more.

I conclude with this story. A person goes to the next world and has an opportunity to visit heaven and hell. He first goes to hell and sees people looking very angry and unhappy, sitting around a table where there is lots of food. He looks more closely, and observes that the people are not eating. Their elbows are locked in a straight position so they cannot bend their arms to put the food in their mouths. He goes to heaven and sees the same scenario. Heaven looks just like hell: people with straight arms, unable to bend their elbows, sitting around a table where there is lots of food. He looks again, and sees that here everyone is smiling and happy. Soon he perceives the reason for this. Unable to reach the food themselves, the people take turns feeding each other.

About the Author

Melinda Ribner, C.S.W., is the Director and Founder of The Jewish Meditation Circle. She has taught Jewish meditation for over fourteen years at numerous synagogues of all affiliations in the United States and Canada, at national conferences of Jewish learning such as Elat Chayim in Accord, New York, C.A.G.E. and Jewish Educators Assembly, and at respected New Age health centers like Kripalu Center for Yoga and Health, Interface in Boston, and The Open Center in New York. She has taught at Jewish academic institutions such as Hebrew Union College and the Jewish Theological Seminary, and at Jewish community organizations such as Lubavitch Women's Organizations, Hadassah, National Council of Jewish Women, and many others.

Melinda, also known as Mindy, received a nonrabbinical ordination to teach Jewish meditation from the legendary Rabbi Shlomo Carlebach that was witnessed by Rabbi Yidel Stein and Rabbi Dr. Seymour Applebaum, both of whom are Orthodox rabbis.

Additionally, she is a certified social worker and a psychotherapist in private practice and at a psychiatric clinic, where she uses meditation as a treatment modality.